Jane Slade of Po

The inspiration for Daphne du Maurier's first novel

Julia
Very best wishes
from Helen Doe
Saga Ruby   April 2007

Helen Doe

Truran

First published in 2002 by Truran, Croft Prince, Mount Hawke, Truro, Cornwall TR4 8EE
www.truranbooks.co.uk

ISBN 1 85022 162 6

Printed and bound in Cornwall by
R. Booth Ltd, Antron Hill, Mabe, Penryn, Cornwall TR10 9HH

To my husband Michael, with love

The Jane Slade *as*
Daphne found her in
1922/23
(FS H*unkin*)

Author's Introduction and Acknowledgements

This book has it roots in a letter written to Daphne du Maurier in 1968. Her kind and very helpful reply started me on a lengthy trail to discover the real people, my family, behind the fiction - a task hindered by a lack of any surviving papers. I have met and corresponded with many people, all of whom have been generous in their encouragement and assistance with information and material. It has been a privilege to meet so many individuals in all walks of life who have given me help and assistance, some of whom are no longer here.

Christian du Maurier Browning has been constant and generous in his help and encouragement with the particularly special bonus of having his beautiful photographs of Polruan in this book; a modern link between the two families.

There are many individuals who have provided information, inspiration, and illustrations, corrected my facts and given me enormous encouragement. Three who will not be able to see the finished result are my mother, Gladys (always known as Gee), her brother David and her sister, Pat. Today's family members who have made large contributions are my aunt, Joan Adams who has kept the few family letters that remain and my cousin, John Adams and his wife, Moya. I owe a permanent debt to Isabel Pickering, who told me many years ago that I should write a book, for her generosity with information. An amazing resource of knowledge and support has come from those I have met through the South West Maritime History Society and maritime conferences: David Clement, Tony Pawlyn, John Bartlett, Malcolm Darch, Mike Stammers, Alston Kennerly and many others. George Hogg, Hon Curator of the Cornwall Maritime Museum has been especially helpful with his advice and took time out of a frantic schedule to read my manuscript and check the details. The staff in the Cornwall County Record Office, the Public Record Office at Kew, the National Newspaper Collection at Colindale, the Royal Institution of Cornwall, the Cornwall Archaeology Unit, the Bodmin Probate office, the Memorial University of Newfoundland and Captain Mike Sutherland and his staff at the Fowey Harbour office have been very helpful. Photographs and information have been generously provided by Stuart Hunkin, John Beaven, Michael Martyn, Wendy Baker, Paul Fenwick, Paul Richards, Brian Hall, Tessa Williams, Jim Matthews, Michael Messenger, the late Jack Samuels, Tony Samuels, Pat Bate, Carole Vivian and the late CH Ward-Jackson. Adam Luck of St Austell Ales allowed me access to their documents. My many friends in Polruan, Fowey and elsewhere have been such great enthusiasts. Last, but not least my thanks go to Michael, my husband; his understanding, patience and support have made this book possible.

This book tells the story of one family in a time of change; they represent many others like them. Any errors or assumptions made in this book are wholly my responsibility. I welcome any comment, addition or correction to the material. The book is a family history and does not have any pretensions to be analytical, or academic.

Helen Doe, Polruan 2002

CONTENTS

Swiss Cottage, Bodinnick before 1920, later renamed Ferryside by the du Mauriers (Author)

INTRODUCTION

Seventy years have passed since Daphne du Maurier wrote her first novel *The Loving Spirit*. My mother came with her family to Cornwall in the late twenties and they bought Ferryside, a former boatyard, in Bodinnick-by-Fowey.

Here she was to find the freedom to write, to walk, to pull a boat, to be alone. It was on one of her walks up Pont Creek, on the estuary separating Bodinnick from Fowey, that she discovered a derelict schooner, the *Jane Slade*. This inspired the first book.

During those early years at Bodinnick, my mother was touched by the kindness of everyone in the village, but it was Harry Adams from Polruan who became her firmest friend and taught her to love and respect the sea. Adams was married to the granddaughter of the real Jane Slade after whom the schooner had been named, and it was he who provided my mother with the letters and papers relating to the Slade family history, their shipbuilding business and their lives in and around Polruan from the 1830s until the 1920s.

The old ship, the family who had built her, the men who had sailed in her, and their wives and lovers obsessed the young Daphne. On a terrible, wild day in October 1930, sitting in her bedroom at Ferryside, she started to write her story. It was, of course, a novel, not a true account of the Slade family. Obviously, names were changed and places invented but it became a very popular book when published in 1931 and launched Daphne's career as a professional writer. Its success gave her what she yearned for most in life, her independence.

Now, seventy years on, another fiercely independent lady still looks out from Ferryside across the harbour towards the open sea, the figurehead of Jane Slade, rescued from the abandoned schooner and given to my mother by Harry Adams all those years ago. I feel certain that if the real Jane Slade's loving spirit were among us today, she would be pleased and proud that her great, great granddaughter has now written the true story of the Slade family of Polruan.

Helen Doe, carefully and movingly, explores her forebears' lives, and the hopes, the fears, the joys and despairs of this once famous family of shipbuilders and master mariners.

Christian du Maurier Browning

Prologue

Everyone stares at Jane. She catches their eye as they pass backwards and forwards on the car ferry between Fowey and Bodinnick. The sightseers in small boats exploring the harbour and the crews on the china clay ships pause to look at her. She raises questions in their minds as she leans against the corner of the house. Who is she? Why is she there? She is used to the stares. She has been admired for many years. She has travelled far from her native Cornwall. Professional and amateur artists have painted her and photographs have been taken. She has inspired and led others and now after her distant travels she seems content and calm watching the ships and yachts leave the port which has always been her home. Jane rests, newly restored to her original colours, above the harbour.

She leans beyond them all, a little white figure with her hands at her breast, her chin in the air, her eyes gazing towards the sea.

Seventy years ago her career seemed over. The ship the *Jane Slade*, whose figurehead she was, had been abandoned, left to rot in the mud of a tidal creek. Pont Creek is a place of rare beauty. There are no houses on the banks in this part of the creek and the trees come right down to the water's edge, giving it a quiet magical peace. There are kingfishers, swans and herons which move elegantly and majestically in search of their food, just as in the 1920s, when there was no one to disturb the explorations of a visitor who was curious about the ship and the figurehead.

The visitor was an aspiring writer, Daphne du Maurier who had finally been given permission to stay alone in their holiday home in Bodinnick. Daphne revelled in her new freedom and avidly explored the local area. She discovered the creek where Jane's small still figure caught her eye and stimulated her imagination. Jane fascinated her, what was she like, what about her family?

Was it true that Jane dominated them all, even after her death......I could think of nothing but Jane Slade.

She asked questions, looked at documents, explored churchyards, read books on merchant sailing ships and the experience of the men who sailed on them. From this came the inspiration for Daphne du Maurier's first novel *The Loving Spirit*: an epic novel of several generations of a shipbuilding and seafaring family dominated by the life and spirit of one woman, Janet Coombe. The novel was published on both sides of the Atlantic; it made du Maurier's name as a writer, gave her the independence to pursue her writing career and even brought her a husband. Major 'Tommy Browning', later Lt. General, read the book and asked to meet the author. When eventually the *Jane Slade* was broken up, the figurehead was given to Daphne - she placed it against the wall of her Bodinnick house where it has remained ever since. All these facts are well known to anyone reading one of the many books on Daphne's life. But who was the woman who had a ship named for her and who inspired such curiosity then and now, who was the real Jane Slade?

Jane is my great great grandmother and this is her story.

Pont Creek is still a place of rare beauty as photographed by Daphne du Maurier's son Christian (Christian du Maurier Browning)

SLADE FAMILY TREE

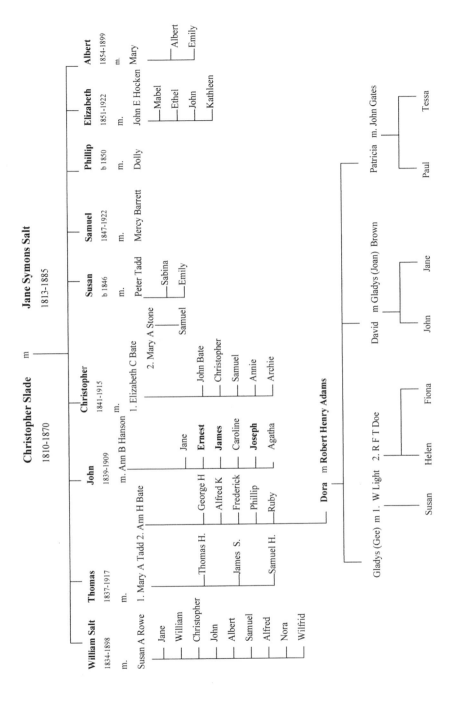

Christopher Slade
1810-1870

m

Jane Symons Salt
1813-1885

William Salt
1834-1898

m.

Susan A Rowe

- Jane
- William
- Christopher
- John
- Albert
- Samuel
- Alfred
- Nora
- Wilfrid

Thomas
1837-1917

m.

1. Mary A Tadd 2. Ann H Bate

- Thomas H.
- James S.
- Samuel H.

John
1839-1909

m. Ann B Hanson

- George H
- Alfred K
- Frederick
- Phillip
- Ruby

- Jane
- **Ernest**
- **James**
- Caroline
- **Joseph**
- Agatha

- **Dora** m **Robert Henry Adams**

Christopher
1841-1915

m.

1. Elizabeth C Bate
2. Mary A Stone

- Samuel

- John Bate
- Christopher
- Samuel
- Annie
- Archie

Susan
b 1846

m.

Peter Tadd

- Sabina
- Emily

Samuel
1847-1922

m.

Mercy Barrett

Phillip
b 1850

m.

Dolly

Elizabeth
1851-1922

m.

John E Hocken Mary

- Mabel
- Ethel
- John
- Kathleen

Albert
1854-1899

- Albert
- Emily

Gladys (Gee) m 1. W Light 2. R F T Doe

- Susan
- Helen
- Fiona

David m Gladys (Joan) Brown

- John
- Jane

Patricia m. John Gates

- Paul
- Tessa

10

1
Jane and Christopher

Softly the bells pealed over the hill from Lanoc Church - then louder; ringing through the air
Janie - where are you to?
She rose from the window, and went away down where the wedding guests were waiting

Just above the secluded creek of Pont in the harbour of Fowey, is Lanteglos church, dedicated to St Wyllow. It stands alone above the creek, next to a farm. The church is placed centrally, but distant from the villages and hamlets of Polruan, Pont, and Bodinnick, which it serves. Here in October 1831, Jane Symons Salt married Christopher Slade.

Jane was eighteen years old when she married. Her father, William Salt, was a mariner from the village of Polruan, her mother, Catherine Symons, was also from a local family. By contemporary standards, Captain Salt was comfortably situated owning several properties and land in the village. Some of this had been inherited; the Salts were an old Polruan family, who could trace their roots back several generations. Jane had been brought up in the village with her brother and four sisters.

What was life like in the village at the beginning of the 19th century? Polruan was described then as a fishing village, but its inhabitants valued a good education for both the girls and the boys. Jane's education seems to have been sound, it certainly was to fit her well for her future life. When she was out of lessons or free from helping her mother in the house, Jane was able to explore. Polruan was, and still is, a small village, clinging onto the steep side of the river Fowey. The houses are built close together with narrow streets and passages between them. There are footpaths criss-crossing the village, sometimes through neighbouring gardens and orchards. Many of the paths lead down to the harbour and the quay. For Jane and her contemporaries, exploring the alleyways and paths would have had the same fascination as it does for the local children today. The harbour is a magnet and Jane, just like all the previous and successive generations, would have spent time on the town quay watching the constant activity of people and ships. Close to the quay was a small shipyard where William Geach and his son, also called William, built small craft, mainly for local use by the fishermen and coastal traders. Plenty of activity was going on in the yard and there would be the thrill of a vessel being launched into the water. If the excitement in the harbour palled, then there were the cliffs, the woods and the paths leading through the countryside. Everyone knew each other and children could explore in safety.

Jane's husband, Christopher, was twenty-one. He had been born in the agricultural village of Pelynt, about eight miles inland to the east of Polruan. His family had lived there for several generations, moving from the neighbouring parish of Duloe around

1700. Christopher's father, Thomas, owned the Axe Inn (now called the Jubilee Inn) together with several other properties in the village and they also farmed in the Pelynt area, (farms called Windsor and Trelay). They were a large family, four sons and five daughters. As the fourth child and third son, Christopher's opportunities for employment in the small rural community of Pelynt would have been limited. His elder brother, John, would take over the running of the Axe Inn and his other brothers went into farming. Christopher had to look for other opportunities and if he looked to the coast, he would have seen the changes - changes that could bring opportunities for a young man.

When Jane and Christopher were born, England was still at war with France. During the various wars, the small locally-built Fowey vessels were employed mainly in the coastal trade, with occasional hazardous visits to the Mediterranean. With bad roads and no railways, all imports into Cornwall were by sea. Key exports were tin and copper from the nearby mines and the china clay trade was just beginning. However, one of the busiest trades for this part of Cornwall had been in carrying contraband from Guernsey and Roscoff in the Channel Islands. High taxes on imports had encouraged the trade and it had long been a traditional way of supplementing low incomes. The shipbuilders in Polruan, Fowey, Mevagissey and Polperro built many ships that were caught in the act of smuggling. The Salt family, as local pilots, would have been well aware of, and quite probably linked to, the trade. Even at inland Pelynt, the Slade family would not have been remote from it. Illicit cargoes were known to have moved up to Pelynt Pool from the coast and as the Slade family owned the only Pelynt inn, they no doubt welcomed some extra supplies. By the time, Christopher and Jane had reached their teens with the lifting of punitive taxation, increased coastguard activity and greater trading opportunities, the smuggling trade was declining.

East Street, Polruan today. The white house on the right and below was where Geach had his yard, where Christopher was apprenticed (Christian du Maurier Browning)

Legitimate trade brought other opportunities; activity increased along the coasts of Cornwall as small shipbuilders worked hard to meet demand for merchant vessels. With war over and the trade routes fully open, a different kind of craft was being built. Larger ships were needed to carry larger and heavier cargoes, but the need for speed was still essential even if it was no longer for outrunning the revenue men.

By the time Christopher was fourteen, the usual age for a young man to start employment, carpenters, shipwrights and blacksmiths were in demand. Christopher would have walked from Pelynt to Polruan with his father to begin his seven years as an apprentice shipwright. He arrived in Polruan at a time of tremendous expansion in shipbuilding. An analysis of the Port registers shows that during 1816-40, in Polruan and in the nearby hamlet of Bodinnick alone, 33 ships with an average tonnage of 68 were built compared to six ships of 41-tons during the previous 30 years. On the other side of the harbour, the Fowey shipbuilders built 39 ships during this time with lower average tonnage of 39. Polruan was the place to be for a young man of ambition. The noise of hammers, saws and caulking mallets were to reverberate around the harbour on an almost constant basis for over 100 years.

Christopher's father had to sign the apprenticeship indentures and the terms agreed were that the boy had *of his own free will and by the consent of his father put himself apprentice* to the shipbuilders. *To learn their art and to serve as an apprentice until the full term and end of seven years. During this term to serve his master faithfully, keep their secrets and keep their lawful commands everywhere gladly do.*

In return for the teaching, the apprentice had to abide by some strict rules:
He *shall do no damage to his masters.*

He shall not waste their goods nor lend them unlawfully to any others.

He shall not commit fornication nor contract matrimony within the said term.

He shall not play at cards or Dice tables or any other unlawful games whereby his master shall have any loss with their own goods or others during said term without licence of his said masters.

He shall neither buy nor sell.

He shall not haunt taverns or playhouses nor absent himself from his said master's service day and night unlawfully.

There is no firm evidence of where Christopher served his apprenticeship, but all the clues point to his starting at the age of fourteen with William Geach, at that time the main shipbuilder in Polruan.

Marriage

Christopher was constrained, amongst other things, from marrying until he had completed his apprenticeship. In 1831, at the age of 21, he was at last free to do so. In the parish registers of Lanteglos in October, the couple are noted as 'both of this parish' and married with 'consent of their parents'. The witnesses were Jane's father, William Salt and Christopher's brother, John Slade. Jane was already carrying their first child. Just two months later, in December, a son, William Salt Slade was born, but he did not live and was buried the same month. Their happiness in their marriage was overtaken by the distress of their first child's death.

Jane's father, William Salt, owned a property in West Street in Polruan and at about the time of his daughter's marriage, he opened a new public house. Perhaps this was to take advantage of the increasing population in the village as the Lugger Inn was in existence on the quay and Mrs Woon also had a public house called The Stag, in West Street. William's pub was named the Russell Inn, after Lord Russell who had done so much to bring about the Reform Act that was eventually passed in 1832. At the time, this must have been a strong statement of radical support. William installed his daughter and new son-in-law to manage the business and in 1832, Christopher Slade of the Russell Inn is first noted as supplying beer for a meeting of the Polruan Town Trust. This may look on the surface like a change of career direction for Christopher, but the reality was different. When one year later, Jane gave birth to her second child, a son named Thomas, her husband gave his occupation as shipwright at the baptism.

Christopher was the official landlord of the Russell Inn, but it was his capable wife, Jane who ran the business. Christopher was unlikely to have given up seven years' hard work qualifying as a skilled craftsman. As a shipwright, he had valuable skills. Business in the port of Fowey was continuing to expand and the local newspapers reported increasing numbers of new ships being launched. Being a shipwright and also being a landlord were to have benefits in several ways. Local inns were valuable places for business information; shipwrights, ship builders, master mariners, local tradesmen and

The Axe Inn, Pelynt, now the Jubilee Inn, which the Slades ran for many years (Miss Mary Maddever)

fishermen all congregated there. For instance, in London, it was the local landlords who were the main suppliers of labour to the docks. As trade in and out of the harbour of Fowey began to expand, new opportunities arose for ambitious businessmen.

The Shipbuilders in Polruan

William Geach and his son had been the shipbuilders on the east side of the river Fowey for some years; the first ship attributed to them was registered in 1789, the 59 ton sloop *Good Intent*. Official registration of local ships had only commenced a few years before in 1786, so it is quite probable that Geach and Son had been building ships prior to this date. As an independent shipwright, Christopher could work for any of the shipbuilders in the port, and there were several firms in operation across the harbour. The likelihood is that he remained in Polruan with Geach and Son, close to home and his family. Christopher and Jane had experienced further sadness when their second child, Thomas, died at the age of four years. Confusingly, as was the custom of the time, their next sons were given the same names; by 1837 they had three year old, William Salt, and one year old Thomas.

While the Slades brought up their young family, Christopher's employers were experiencing business problems. In 1837, William Geach and Son were declared bankrupt, and the yard and contents put up for sale. The notice in the paper detailed the auction of their investments in local ships.

Royal Cornwall Gazette 1837 17th February. To be sold by Public Auction, by order of the Assignees of William Geach the Elder, William Geach the Younger, Bankrupts, at the undermentioned times and places respectively, viz.; at the Ship Inn, Fowey on Monday the 20th of February inst. at 2:00 in the Afternoon

> *1/16 Part or Share in the Schooner*
> > *'Speculation', reg. 70 ton, James Geach, Master*
> *1/16 Shares in the Sloops*
> > *'Cornish Trader', 40 ton, Jacob Beer, Master;.*
> > *'Lively', James Geach, Master*
> > *'Spring', 60 ton, Richard Scantlebury, Master;*
> > *'Glory', 60 ton, William Salt, Master;*
> > *'Four Friends', 80 tons, Thomas Scantlebury, Master*
> > *'Fanny', 70 tons, Philip Pill, Master;*
> > *'Flower', 60 tons, James Tippett, Master;*
> > *'Newhouse', 90 tons, Peter Tadd, Master;*
> > *'Rose', 60 tons, Benjamin Brokenshaw, Master*
> *1/16 and 1/32 in the sloop*
> > *'Charlotte Ann', 76 tons, Robert Pearne, Master*
> *3/16 and 1/32 in the sloop*
> > *'Elizabeth and Ann', 66 tons, Charles Hodge, Master*

All the above vessels belong to the Port of Fowey, are substantially built, and well found in stores of all descriptions and all at Sea, and expected in Port daily.

It then went on to describe their stock in trade:

At the SHIPWRIGHT'S YARDS in Polruan, on Tuesday the 21st, precisely at 1:00, several hundred feet of Oak, Elm, and Bulk Timber, quantity of Oak Plank, several dozen Spars, 5 very good Pilchard drift Nets, several Boats, Shipwright's Tools, Steamers, Boilers, some Thousand Trenails, Vessel Moulds, Fire Wood, etc.

At the DWELLING HOUSE and STORE ROOMS in Polruan, on Wednesday the 22nd and following days, precisely at one, a quantity of Groceries, Drapery, Hardware, Drugs, Oils, various Paints, Nails, Pitch, Tar, Salt, Coals, Ovens, Bricks, Carpentry tools, ad all the HOUSEHOLD FURNITURE, comprising Mahogany and other Tables and Chairs, Sofa, Mahogany Chest of Drawers, an excellent eight day Clock, China, Glass and all other articles of Household Furniture. The above Property which is well worth the Public attention, will be SOLD in convenient Lots to the best Bidder, under the Fiat of Bankruptcy...

The list gives some typical contents of a yard of the time. It shows the wood waiting for a new ship to be built or existing ships to be repaired, the trenails (oak pins, used in place of nails, to secure the planking), the pilchard nets, (fishing was still an essential part of the local economy), and the other items of chandlery from ovens to paints.

While the failure was unfortunate for the Geach family and their creditors, it was an opportunity for new shipbuilding businesses to start and others to expand. John Marks and William Rendle, originally from Looe, were brothers-in-law and had been co-partners in shipbuilding since 1826. Marks was based in Bodinnick, up river and in 1837, just as Geach went bankrupt, Rendle moved to Polruan to rent a yard in West Street. At about the same time, Nicholas Butson, who had previously been a shipwright with Geach, also set up as a shipbuilder and evidence suggests that Christopher may have continued working with Butson.

The shares in ships listed in the bankruptcy of Geach and Son illustrates the method by which risk was shared in the significant cost of building and running ships. The smaller ships had required just a few shareholders, but as these ships became bigger, with higher costs of building and equipping, ownership was spread and many members of the local community owned shares in them. There could be a maximum of 64 shares per vessel and the registers of the shareowners show the names and occupations of these local investors. Not only were ships being built locally, but also ships were purchased from elsewhere and registered in the port. Timber was in short supply and Canadian-built ships were already arriving to be adapted in the local yards for deep sea trading. These Canadian ships were being built in timber-rich Newfoundland by North

Devon men. The wide shareholding meant that the future of the ship, its prosperity and the men who sailed in her became closely linked with the fortunes of these communities who invested not just their labour, but now their money as well. Christopher was among the local people who had sufficient income to invest.

Christopher's first investment was the *Levant Star*, a snow of 147-tons built in Merioneth in 1819. In the Port register, he is described as a victualler with two of the sixty-four shares in 1835. It is noticeable that when he invested in ships built by Rendle (two shares in the 53-ton sloop *Ranger* in 1839 and four shares in the 66-ton schooner, *Rachael Anne* in 1841) his occupation is victualler. His occupation when registering his shares in Butson built ships, for instance the 68-ton *Alert* in 1842, is shipwright. Indicating perhaps that this was a ship on which he had worked. It was also possible to invest in kind by providing goods or labour: continued share ownership needed money. If Christopher also had an ambition to build his own ships then he was certainly going to need larger amounts of capital or a business partner.

On 15th December 1839 at Pelynt Christopher Slade's father, Thomas, died at the age of 65. In his will, made ten days earlier, he left two leasehold properties in Pelynt to his shipwright son. Christopher had little use for property in Pelynt and at least one of them was sold to his brother:

In 6 May 1840 Assignment of Grylls Tenement in Pelynt Church Town.
Between Mr Christopher Slade of Polruan, shipwright and John Slade of Pelynt, Innkeeper. Consideration of £57.10 shillings

This brought in some capital and, although relatively small, would have been of some assistance towards the plan that Christopher and his father-in-law, Captain William Salt, had developed. Just below the Russell Inn, on the waterfront, William had a piece of land and here in 1841 he built a shipwright's yard. This caused a complaint from his

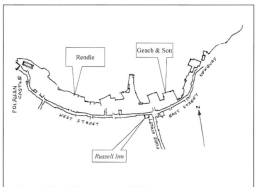

Occupiers of Polruan Yards c1842

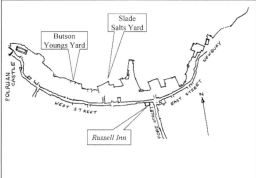

Occupiers of Polruan Yards c1850

neighbour, Mary Hicks, in 1840 that Captain Salt had taken stone from her and Mr Rashleigh's land to build his yard. William was forced to pay compensation. However, the 1841 tithe map shows the tenant as Nicholas Borlase, a sailmaker. Why did they rent the new shipyard to someone else? The answer is that it may not, after all, have been the right time to start a new venture.

The 'Hungry Forties'

The 1840s were a time of severe economic depression in Cornwall. The towns and villages were poor places; the wealth from the mines and china clay quarries often bypassed the residents. There were riots in the streets as men were out of work and the farmers were badly hit by the same potato blight which was affecting Ireland. Shipbuilding slowed down and in 1841 and again in 1842, the shipwright's yard leased by Rendle, called Youngs yard, in West Street, Polruan was for sale.

In the 1841 census, Christopher gave his occupation as publican; he and Jane now had four sons, William, Thomas, John and one-month-old, Christopher junior. In May, the next year the 68-ton schooner *Alert* was launched from Butsons yard. The largest single shareholder was William Salt with fourteen shares and Christopher, occupation shipwright, had five shares. The shareholding in the *Alert* shows the range of local occupations connected with shipbuilding: merchant, blockmaker (the blocks are the wooden pulleys used in the running rigging) and ropemaker. This was a typical shareholding pattern of the time. Christopher was to take a keen interest in the *Alert*.

Alert   May 1842
ON: 11411 Tons: 68 Rig: Schooner Square sterned   Dim: 60 x 16 x 9 Builder: Butson

Shares	Name	Occupation	Residence
9	J M Carnall	Sailmaker	Fowey
14	William Salt	Mariner	Polruan
2	Phillip Salt	Mariner	Polruan
5	James Bray	Blacksmith	Polruan
6	William Abbott	Baker	Polruan
5	Christopher Slade	Shipwright	Polruan
4	Nicholas Butson	Shipbuilder	Polruan
1	James Tippett	Mariner	Polruan
9	John Knight	Merchant	Lostwithiel
1	Charles Lacey	Blockmaker	Fowey
2	Sam Buller	Butcher	Fowey
2	Mary Whitford	Spinster	Fowey
2	Edward Thomas	Ropemaker	Fowey
2	Edward Strike	Shipbroker	Fowey

The *Alert* was Nicholas Butson's last ship; he died in 1844 at the age of sixty-six and his two sons took over his yard. Over the next few years the number of new ships fell dramatically and there was a shake up in the number and ownership of the shipbuilding yards. Giving a completely clear list, of which builder built which ship and in which yard, is fraught with difficulties. The register of ships for the Port of Fowey shows the names of some of the builders, but not on all ships especially those from the earlier years. The newspaper articles are more informative on some ships, but their accuracy of reporting cannot be relied upon. It was not unusual for a builder to use space in another's yard when his own was inadequate or had become unavailable for some reason. Workmen as well as space were changed and changed about from one employer to another according to need. There are two very useful sources for Polruan at this time. In 1841 there was a tithe map drawn up. This showed all the properties in Polruan subject to tithes and the owners and lessees. Add to this the Land Tax assessments, and it is possible to track annual changes of occupier and owner.

There is evidence of this shifting of the waterfront properties. Even William Geach and his son, last heard of as bankrupts in 1831 came back onto the scene briefly. The Land Tax shows that John Carnall owned Youngs yard in West Street. Based in Fowey, he had been the port's principal sailmaker for many years. He could have acquired this yard on the bankruptcy of Geach since he would have been one of the main creditors.

With Nicholas Butson's death, his sons, Nicholas and Joseph, continued the business and were based at Youngs yard in West Street. These were difficult trading times, the output from Butsons yard fell and they built just four ships of average size 36-tons over a period of ten years. They had taken the site over from William Rendle. Marks and Rendle had built their last ship, the 80-ton coastal schooner *William West*, in 1846.

Polruan waterfront - still showing the continuing existance of shipyards (Christian du Maurier Browning)

The view of the harbour mouth from the headland, Polruan, where Jane/Janet could view the ships entering and leaving port (Christian du Maurier Browning)

Rendle seems to have gone out of business then, but remained in Polruan until 1853 when he died. His brother-in-law and partner, John Marks remained at Bodinnick where in 1848 he built a new horse boat for the Bodinnick to Fowey crossing, but after this, he and his family disappear from local records. The yard at Bodinnick was later taken over by George Nickels, a Fowey shipbuilder. The Geachs' brief foray back into running a yard ended in 1845 when they sold all their sites to John Hicks.

Through the economic recession of 1840s the shipbuilding businesses in Polruan were clearly in a state of flux, causing employment problems for shipwrights and carpenters and related businesses. Many Cornish people took the opportunity to leave the area for better opportunities. The recession encouraged many to emigrate, ships sailed regularly to Canada and the USA. Smuggling activity was once again reported and in a poignant example of the tragedy that was affecting Cornwall's rural poor, the *Royal Cornwall Gazette* published a recipe from the Royal Agricultural Improvement Society of Ireland. It described how to make wholesome food from diseased potatoes. Throughout it all Jane continued to run the Russell Inn. She had assistance in this and help with her growing family from a large support network of nieces, from Polruan and from Pelynt. The innkeeping business remained a constant source of steady and essential income.

Jane's father, William, was the harbourmaster for Fowey harbour, a position then that was mainly concerned with collecting dues from the ships using the harbour. He had held this position under licence from Lostwithiel since 1837. The harbour rights were historically owned by Lostwithiel Corporation despite the fact that Lostwithiel was five miles up river. The Corporation licensed the right to collect the harbour dues to the highest bidder, normally for period of seven years. The harbourmaster could make good use of his role to make suitable recommendations. Ships arriving in the port that were in need of some repairs, could be recommended to a suitable yard, perhaps to one where his son-in-law worked.

One highlight in the difficult times was the recognition given to Fowey by royalty. Queen Victoria and Prince Albert provided the local residents with a moment of great excitement when they arrived in the harbour on an official visit on the 11th September, 1846. They entered the harbour at half-past ten and went ashore, the royal party transferring to carriages to visit the mines in the neighbourhood, even venturing underground. They then returned to visit Mr. JT Treffry at his home, Place, in the centre of Fowey. The party finally returned to their yacht and left early that evening for Plymouth. The Harbourmaster of Fowey would have been at the forefront of the occasion, overseeing moorings, the conveying of the Royal party to and from the quay at Broad Slip. The harbour would have been full of vessels of all sizes crowded with onlookers hoping to catch a glimpse of the Queen and Prince Regent. Jane and Christopher would have been no exception to the curiosity and excitement which gripped the community.

Thrilling though this was, it could not change the bad fortune that was affecting the whole area: the pilchard season was poor, harvests failed in wet weather, potato blight reoccurred in 1847, miners went on strike, and cholera arrived in Mevagissey a few miles along the coast. Such was the terror engendered by this disease that when a fishing boat from Mevagissey put into Fowey with a sick man, the inhabitants of Fowey refused to take him in and ran the boat out of the harbour, threatening to shoot the men on board.

Slades Yard

1847 was the end of the recession, Christopher at the age of 37 together with his father-in-law, William, finally set up a shipbuilding yard. They had their site, built six years previously, but they still needed capital. A new shipbuilding venture required wood, tools, men and some simple buildings. William used his main asset, the Russell Inn and took out a mortgage on it of £200.

For the first time, Christopher was listed as a Polruan shipbuilder, buying two shares in *Fancy*, 62-ton sloop built by Geach in 1825, plus four shares in *Louisa*, 66-ton sloop built by Marks and Rendle in 1839. There are, however no new ships attributable to Christopher's yard at this time. He may have started the business by handling repair work, a constant requirement for ships from the time they were launched. He increased his buying, spending larger amounts, often with William Salt, in acquiring ships from elsewhere. In 1850, Christopher bought all sixty-four shares in a Devon-built schooner *Brilliant*, 68-tons, subsequently selling 16 each to Samuel Climo who became her master and to William. Either Christopher or William would have travelled to examine the ship and then after purchase brought her back for the necessary repairs, conversion work and re-rigging at their yard before selling her.

By 1851, the year of the Great Exhibition, the economy was growing. Polruan could no longer be described as a fishing village. The population had increased significantly with a large number of families moving in from the local villages. Less than half of the Polruan residents in 1851 had been born in the village. The number of occupations related to shipbuilding or men described as mariners now outnumbered the agriculturists. There are four shipbuilders listed in the census for Polruan and all of them were living in West Street. There were the two brothers, Joseph and Nicholas Butson, described as Master Shipbuilders, employing three apprentices. William Rendle, aged 52 still gave his occupation as shipbuilder and at the Russell Inn was Christopher, aged 41, occupation shipbuilder.

Christopher and Jane's family by now comprised their eldest son, William, who at sixteen gave his occupation as shipbuilder's apprentice and four other sons from Thomas aged fourteen down to Philip aged one. They had one surviving daughter, Susan, aged five. Just a few years before, on 20th October 1844, they had buried a daughter, named Jane after her mother; the baby did not live to see her first birthday. Jane was now pregnant again and on 29th December 1851 Elizabeth Anne was baptised at the parish church of Lanteglos.

As 1852 began, Jane and Christopher and their young family had come through the recession, the Russell Inn had been established for twenty years and Christopher with the help of Jane's father, William Salt, had his own yard in which to repair ships. With the death in 1852 of William Rendle, Slades and Butsons became the only ship repair and shipbuilding businesses on the east side of the Fowey River. Christopher began to consider the next step, to move from repair and conversion work to building new schooners and brigantines.

Map showing the Fowey estuary (Sue Lewington)

2
The First Ships

Changes came with the china clay, Plyn was no longer a sleepy harbour but a busy port, with the noise of the ships and the loading of clay. The shipbuilding yard of Thomas Coombe was important in Plyn. Large vessels were launched from the slip now, ships of over 100 tons, schooners

In 1853, the first direct reference was made to the existence of Christopher Slade's yard; on June 24th in a brief, but sad note in the *Royal Cornwall Gazette*:
John Roberts a shipwright of good character fell over steps leading to Mr. Slade's building yard at Polruan on 20th by which he was so much injured as to cause his death. Christopher's name was now also mentioned more frequently in local business matters. He had been the host for the Annual Court Leet at the Russell Inn (the annual meeting of the local manor court) and in 1850, he had been appointed Overseer of the Poor. In 1854, he was renting a cellar on Polruan quay from the Town Trust for coal. With no coal reserves of its own, Cornwall had to import. As an essential energy source for any activity from mining to domestic use, coal had long been part of the trade of the port. It remained the main import to Fowey for many years, while minerals and china clay were the main exports. Christopher's rental of a cellar on the quay in Polruan was important. As the ships unloaded their cargo onto the Polruan quay, the cellar was used for temporary storage and then sold onwards.

In 1854 came Albert, Jane and Christopher's twelfth child. He joined his surviving six brothers and two sisters in the Russell Inn. William and John were working alongside their father at the yard and Christopher junior, was about to join them - with three sons

Lanteglos/Lanoc Church as it is today (Christian du Maurier Browning)

working with Christopher at the yard, it was truly a family business. Their second son Thomas, now seventeen was at sea in his uncle's ship, *Alert*. In the same year that their eldest son, William, became a qualified shipwright, a newly-built ship was launched from the small Slades yard below West Street in April 1856. It was a brigantine, the *Peter and James*, built for Peter Tadd, a local master mariner and owner of several ships.

The other shareholders investing in the ship include Richard Barrett. Polruan now had its own resident sailmaker, previously the sails had been made in Fowey by John Carnall. Another major shareholder was rather more distant, a ship owner from Grangemouth, Scotland, on the banks of the Firth. Robertson's investment was likely to have been linked with trade interests to and from Grangemouth. The success of these investments, for all of the shareholders, was dependent on good weather, a capable master and crew, a well-built ship, a regular supply of cargoes and good fortune. The *Peter &James* lasted for ten years, but was lost with all her crew and papers on passage from Salonica in October 1865.

Christopher did not officially invest in shares in the *Peter & James*; he may have been financially stretched as his next investment was a few months later, in August, when he bought four shares in a Prince Edward Island-built brigantine the *Capella*, 142-tons. This brand new ship had been imported from Newfoundland by Charles Harvey, a Fowey shipowner. Christopher, William Salt, Edward Hocken and Richard Barrett, all Polruan businessmen, bought a large number of the shares in her. Canadian-built ships were purchased and then brought to the local yards to be strengthened and adapted; the work on the *Capella* no doubt was handled by Christopher and his men. Repair work and rebuilding work were the bread and butter income to the yards since the building of new ships were big investments of capital, labour and space. Once started, the skeleton of a new ship in its frame dominated these small yards and it would be many months, sometimes over a year, until it could be launched. In 1858 Christopher launched the *Kate & Anne* for the Hockens, another local shipowning family.

The association between the Slade, Tadd and Hocken families shown in these two ships was to last well into the next century. The three families had moved into Polruan from East Cornwall at much the same time. Here too is the start of another long business association with the name of William Geake, as a shareholder. William's name was later to become significantly associated with several Polruan ships as their managing owner. The *Kate & Anne* was well-built and carefully sailed. She survived until November 1892 when she was sunk in a collision with a steamship, SS *Bovonia* off Milford Haven. Even after this collision, she was later raised and used as a barge in Milford until at least 1974 - an amazing survival of 108 years.

With the yard continually busy, Jane had her hands full with the Russell Inn and her large family. Their last child, Mary Kitty, had been born in February 1856. She was buried, aged nine months, with three of her siblings, in the graveyard at Lanteglos.

While infant mortality rates were high, the death of just one child was a tragedy and Jane had lost four. The business had to be maintained even in a grieving household. Ship auctions were held from the inn, such as the advertisement in on 23rd October 1857 in the *West Briton* for the *Margaret*. However, it was Christopher as the landlord who was fined in 1858 at the local magistrate's court, at Trecan Gate, in March for keeping his house open after proper hours. He was fined 10s with costs. Rural inns could usually be flexible with their opening hours, but there must have been a new policy in force (or a keen local policeman) as two other innkeepers in the area were also fined for the same offence over the next few months.

The Polruan Yards

The demand for larger ships was having an impact on the small Polruan yards. The West Street yards were small and inadequate to house the frames needed for these larger vessels. Launching also required ease of access and the days of building on any patch of beach were long gone. The waterfront of Polruan changed as businesses expanded and moved. The blacksmith, James Bray, had purchased Bennetts House and Quays in East Street, moving down the hill from his previous base in Fore Street, getting closer to the shipbuilding activity. Richard Barrett, the sailmaker was to follow his example in 1862. He moved to the confusingly named Newquay, a quay built to the east of Polruan near Brazen Island. The other Polruan shipbuilders, the Butson brothers, who by now were employing nine men and three boys, had moved to a new yard in 1859.

11 February: On Monday morning last, a landslip took place in the new building yard of Messrs. N. and J. Butson at Polruan, near to which was a vessel almost completely in frame, intended to carry about 200 tons. The earth fell against the shores by which the vessel was supported, starting her 3 feet from her original position; and by falling down in the yard the whole structure became disunited, by which the loss to the builders must be very considerable. But in the midst of this misfortune there is still a consolation, for it is generally believed, that if the land slip had taken place an hour or two later, several lives would have been lost, as the workmen were employed near to the spot where it fell.

The likeliest location is Brazen Island. The shoreline here was used for quarrying and at this time, the small rock of Brazen Island was linked to the shore to provide a base.

Christopher also, took the chance to expand his business, taking over the lease in Butsons old yard below West Street where John Hawken a new blacksmith was based. This gave Christopher access to two yards; new building could be done in one yard and repair work continue in the other. He employed eight men and three boys, including his eldest son, William, as head shipwright working alongside his brothers, John and Christopher junior. Christopher increased his investment in ships, buying more shares in the schooner *Alert*, on which his son, Thomas, had served his early days at sea.

The Polruan yards were very small, and the following quote from the late CH Ward Jackson, puts them into perspective. *Although shipbuilding was probably the most labour intensive industry in the whole country, 20 or so workpeople was about as many as any one of these employed compared with 570 in a yard of average size in the 1830s.* Here he was making a comparison with national yards. *In Padstow, Tredwens Yard in the 1860s covered five acres and could build five vessels at one time. In Polruan, the steep sides of the harbour restricted the size of the yards. They got round this by enlarging where possible out into the harbour but this would never give the same return as flat land. These yards were little more than reclaimed beach where just one vessel could be set up in frame and worked on until it was ready to be slid down to high water. Add a shed or two, perhaps a sawpit and facilities for drying and steaming timber to shape, perhaps a house from which the proprietor might oversee what is going on and you have a shipyard Fowey style. In addition, if no space for timber ponds existed, Pont Pill afforded every bit as well the means of maturing wood chained together in rafts. However, remember that the size of these ships was limited. The famous fast sailing clippers of 1860-1890 were 1,400-tons. A fair size Fowey registered schooner was about 100-tons.*

The Busy Port

The Port of Fowey was becoming very busy and an important development was being debated. A plan had been proposed to build a railway line from Lostwithiel to Fowey, in order to bring china clay more easily into the port for onward export. A newspaper report in the *West Briton* in November 1860 included some estimates of the potential increased shipments out of Fowey and gives an indication of the type of cargoes being loaded.

These circumstances and the necessity for sending the clay to other ports to be re-shipped, have long directed the attention of the clay merchants and others to the advantages of the Port of Fowey. Previous to the opening of the Cornwall Railway, the cost of bringing clay and stone to Fowey was so great that, with the exception of a small quantity that was brought round from Charlestown and elsewhere in lighters for reshipment, nothing was done to turn these advantages to account.

On the completion of the proposed line, however, more, especially in conjunction with the contemplated branch to the Clay Works of St. Stephens, there is every reason to believe that the bulk of China Clay and stone will be shipped from the port of Fowey in addition to the timber, ore, and other merchandize, of which, the estimated traffic is as follows:

Iron Ore	14,000	Coal culm	6,000
General merchandize	3,000	Iron, Brick, and Manures	2,000
Timber	12,000	China Clay and Stone	33,000
Lime and limestone	6,000		

Polruan Quay on the left and the remains of the Coal Wharf on the right (Christian du Maurier Browning)

If the exports were the china clay and stone and the iron ore, then the gap between the imports and exports was significant; an import tonnage of 29000 and an export of 47000. This meant that a high proportion of ships were arriving in ballast.

This increasing volume of trade was leading to complaints about the Lostwithiel Corporation, which was seen as an indifferent landlord. Pressure was mounting to control matters more locally - a step that Christopher was likely to support since the neglect was causing local shipowners considerable problems. He rented the town quay at Polruan and received fees for all merchandise landed there; anything that made it easier to bring ships alongside would have found favour. His father-in-law, William Salt, was no longer the harbourmaster having been removed from the post in 1856. In 1860, a Fowey resident, William Hewett wrote a letter of complaint:

28 Dec West Briton: Sir,-Since the appearance of the letter on the above subject in a recent West Briton, Mr. Brokenshire, of this town, as the owner of a vessel, has been summoned to answer the charge of throwing ballast on the 'Ballast Quay', within reach of the tide, which he must answer. The assertion made last week that 'The Lostwithiel corporation ought to be fined', finds a confirmation in the fact that the master of the vessel (whose act the owner is called on to answer for) could not throw the ballast anywhere on the said quay, but within reach of the tide; for the water covers it during some springs more than 4 feet. The state of the matter is much worse even than this, for outside the wall of faggots there must be at least more than 100 tons of rubbish, and vessels have been known to be caught there in coming down on tide and turn on their beam ends. There is no constituted authority here, possessing any power to call the corporation to account for mismanagement, which ought certainly to have been the case; and, it is not known that 5s a year are expended for the benefit of the navigation in any way. Stones, dangerous to vessels grounding on the beaches, are left to lie there, and thousands of tons of rubbish and mud lying close to the town, and allowed to remain, and accommodation for landing is unattended.

The twin pressures, of the silting up of the harbour and the need for the ships to dispose of their ballast before loading the cargo, would continue for many years. Ships needed to take ballast on board when they were empty; ballast was any material (usually stones or gravel) that could be loaded in order to ensure that the ship could sail safely when empty. When they subsequently picked up a cargo the ballast had to be unloaded speedily. But before the debate on the rights of the harbour was resolved, another dispute was to directly involve Christopher.

Christopher

What type of man was Christopher? Was he as ambitious as his business growth suggests? There are no papers that survive to give any wider view of his personality. The only mention of him is in a letter written to defend him. It was written by a good friend, Captain William Smith, and related to a dispute over the Polruan ferry, an open rowing boat that plied the route between Polruan and Fowey. In dispute were the exclusive rights to carry passengers between the two communities. On the one side with the ancient rights of the Lady of the Manor, was Lady Grenville, her agent, William Pease and her lessee, Peter Tadd. On the other side was the sacked boatman, Tommy Hill, who had set up in a rival boat for himself with the support of a local man, Thomas Tadd (who just happened to be Peter Tadd's estranged brother). Most of Polruan found itself divided between the warring parties and many no doubt enjoyed the entertainment it provided.

Christopher, as lessee of the Polruan quay, found himself drawn into this in 1863. In addition to the rental of the coal cellar, he had the franchise for the main quay, receiving the rentals and dues from all the users. His reputation had to be defended by Captain Smith who was writing to Lady Grenville's land agent, William Pease. It appears that complaints had been made about the ferryman landing passengers at the main quay in Polruan where Christopher had his coal cellar. There may have been some obstruction in the work of unloading the ships or simply a refusal to pay dues.

Polruan 3rd December 1863.

Mr Wmm Pease
Dear Sir
I duly received your letter this morning of yesterday's date and note its contents. I think you are wrong informed about Mr Slade. I have seen him about it and he denies of making use of any language as you state, its true that Mr Slade do rent the Town Quay and receives something as due for all merchandise

that is landed. I holds the Town books that is more than 200 years hold and the town Quay have been let every year to the one that will give the most rent, if you refer to the Map of Polruan you will find that the Town Quay is not the proper landing place its marked another place, landing place. As to my self I have not spoke one word about the ferry I have been .... in all of it but there is still Great Complaints I hear about the accommodation there is an independent Gentleman Farmer that lives at the head of Polruan making a great complaint about the ferry man a five days ago, I dont think that Mr Slade have interfered atawl with the ferryman only he sess no one helst will not alow their children to go in the ferry boat with that man, I can assure you sir that its far from the wish of the inhabitants of Polruan to go to war against Lady Granvill or the Honourable George For they will not profit one farthing by the ferry be as it may and I know and have said if it belongs to every body it will belong to no one and after a little wile there would be no one to attend, but if people goes in opposition the land holder have no power to stop them. I thought it was awl quiet now,
I am sir yours respectfully William Smith.

No further correspondence refers to Christopher, or his language, but the Polruan ferry dispute rumbled on for several more years.

Increasing Number of Ships

The various yards around the port were building and launching a regular supply of new ships. Timber was in constant demand and with the local timber exhausted, ships were arriving from Quebec with timber consignments. Another scarcity was in skilled shipwrights. They were hard to keep, once they had served their apprenticeship, many left to other more prosperous employment areas such as the naval dockyards at Devonport, Portsmouth and Chatham. However, the good news in 1863 was the cutting of the first turf for the Lostwithiel to Fowey railway, with its promise of increased trade for the port.

There is a gap in Christopher's shipbuilding (or at least of the ships attributed to him) of six years. His next ship was the Juno in 1864 and from the share ownership it looks as if Christopher built her in partnership with William Hicks, a local merchant. This investment differentiated Christopher from the other shipbuilders in the port. Most of them would take out two or so shares in their own work, but never as many as twelve.

While Christopher was committed to an investment in sail, steam was continuing to make its presence felt. In 1854 the first steam powered vessel, the Forager had been registered at Fowey to be used as a tug. Built in Nottingham in 1826 she was described as a schooner rigged paddle steamer. In 1864 the West Briton described a local experiment; Messrs. Butson at Fowey are constructing a small steamer, owned by a company in Mevagissey, to be used as a driver for mackerel and pilchards and as a collector in case of calms; so that the fish may be forwarded to the different markets in time. It is an experiment and may be the means of developing fishing resources. No trace has been found of this steamer and the venture may

not have been a successful one. While it was not repeated, the experiment foretold changing times. Meanwhile the local residents continued their investment in sail.

Christopher and his neighbours bought further shares in the *Jane & Ann* in January 1865. This 160-ton brigantine, built in Perth, was registered in Fowey by the Hocken family. This was followed in February of the same year with investments in the 60-ton Dartmouth built schooner, *Isabella*, majority-owned by the Tadd family. Two years later the next new Slade ship was launched. *The Royal Cornwall Gazette* report of her launch on 19th July 1866 highlighted the importance of speed for the owners. Small fast sailing ships could still hold their own against competition from steam.

1866 Jul 19 LAUNCH AT POLRUAN. - *A superior clipper schooner, built by Messrs. Slade and Sons for Captain Hocken, of Polruan, was successfully launched on Thursday. She was named 'The Sparkling Wave', by Miss Jorey, daughter of Mr. Jorey, merchant, of Pentewan, near St Austell. The vessel is intended for the foreign trade, being classed A1 for 12 years, will carry 280 tons, and is likely to be a fast sailer.*

The main investors here were the Reverend Treffry of Place, who had succeeded his uncle as the local squire in Fowey, John Edward Hocken, Christopher and William Luke. Luke was from Charlestown, a significant port for clay exports. Among the shareholders were five master mariners. The *Sparkling Wave* was followed two years later by another new ship, this time for the Tadd family.

1868 August 13 LAUNCH.- A new schooner 'The Silver Stream' 280 tons burthen, classed A1 at Lloyds for 12 years, has been successfully launched from the building yard of Messrs. Slade and Sons, Polruan. The ceremony of christening was performed by Miss Slade. The vessel is to be commanded by Captain Elias R. Tadd, and to be used in the Mediterranean and Brazilian trade.

Christopher, again held a significant shareholding and William Geake, previously a schoolmaster of Dobwalls with investments in other Slade ships, was now starting his career as a managing agent. In this role he acted as an accountant and company secretary for the other shareholders.

1868 was also another year of expansion for Christopher. In addition to the two yards on West Street, he had purchased Bennetts House and Quays in East Street, previously in the occupation of James Bray, the blacksmith. It was a valuable and important site, it had previously been the Geach site where the young apprentice, Christopher, had started. When James Bray had purchased it nine years earlier the description had been:

a most desirable WATERSIDE PROPERTY or shipwrights yard situate in the principal part of the town, and known by the name of Bennetts House and Quays ....extending in breadth 80; in depth 83ft, and having a draught of water 11 ft at spring tides, and 6 ft at neap tides, affording an unparalleled opportunity to parties embarking on any waterside business.

This expansion would enable him to build bigger ships from a more accessible site, right at the centre of activity close to Polruan Town Quay. The yard would need to be extended, the description above gives the depth as 83 feet. By now the ships being built were over 100 feet long. Here they had more space for the various activities. The sawpit, steam chest (for bending the wood to shape) and blacksmith's shed could all be sited safely apart from the inflammable sawdust. On the other side of the yard from the quay was Richard Barrett's sail loft.

The New Harbour Board

The correspondents to the *West Briton* newspaper in 1860, who had complained about the inadequacies of the Lostwithiel Corporation, at last saw their wishes realised. The Fowey Harbour Board was set up by Act of Parliament to regulate the harbour in 1869, taking away control from Lostwithiel. In June 1869, the new railway delivered the first shipment of china clay from Fowey. This opened the harbour considerably. A seamless movement of china clay, by train then straight to the dockside, would make a significant increase in the number of ship using the ports and provide valuable cargoes for Fowey ships out of port. The next few years looked set for prosperity for shipping.

1869 June 24 FOWEY. THE CLAY TRAFFIC- *The brig 'Urania', Capt. Pinkham, has completed loading a cargo of clay which was brought over the Lostwithiel and Fowey Railway. The captain is very much pleased with the arrangements for loading. Vessel drawing 17 feet can lie afloat along the jetty at the lowest spring tides, and Fowey harbour is both safe and commodious.*

Christopher and Jane were now at their most prosperous time, enjoying the success of their various business interests. They still had another ambition to fulfil. For some years Slade and Sons had built ships for other investors. If, however, they built a ship and retained ownership, the profits from the trading activity would be theirs. Christopher and his shipwright sons would design and build the schooner, destined for the profitable fruit trade. Thomas, their second son, now qualified as a master mariner, would be in command. All their many years of experience, on shore and at sea, would go into building this schooner. A start was made in 1868 and she would be due for launching in 1870. The ship was to be named after Jane and the figurehead was to be:

Janet herself, Janet with her dark hair and hands at her breast.

Before she was launched, tragedy hit the family. There was a death but not quite as described in the fictional account, *The Loving Spirit.*

3
Jane Slade & Sons, Shipbuilders

It was Janet who had the first say and the last say at Ivy House, and now it had come to be the same down at the yard. It was Janet who suggested a change here, or an improvement there, it was Janet who ordered this and refused that

Unlike, Janet Coombe, her fictional counterpart, it was not Jane who died but Christopher. He died on 28th February 1870 of heart disease; the death was registered by his second son, Thomas. He was buried in the graveyard at Lanteglos. T*he Royal Cornwall Gazette* on 5th March 1870 announced his death at *age 60, greatly respected.* Christopher's will, drawn up ten years earlier in 1860, left all his property, stock-in-trade as a shipbuilder and innkeeper to be held in trust for his children. All his children were to have equal shares and Jane was to have full use of the Trust during her widowhood. Jane was also named as the executor of his will. As trustees, he chose his brothers John and Samuel from Pelynt, and his friend, William Smith. Despite his efforts in building his business, Christopher neither assumed nor demanded that his sons should follow in his path. *If any of my sons now working with me wish to carry on the business and the trade of ship building, they can do so but the business to be valued as part of the trust and paid out accordingly.* In the age of the stereotypical Victorian autocrat, he made no demands on his children and treated his sons and daughters equally.

His business interests were considerable. He owned or leased four of the five shipbuilding yards in Polruan. He owned Bennetts House and Quay, and rented Newquay dock (now Toms yard, East Street), he rented a yard off West Street from his father in law, Captain Salt, and since 1865 he had been the tenant of Youngs yard in West Street (now Seacroft). The only other Polruan shipbuilder was Butsons and they were based at Brazen Island with a smaller yard at Bodinnick. Christopher had built and launched five ships from his yard, four of which were still on the port's register. He was the tenant of the Russell Inn, had shares in several local ships, was the managing owner of the schooner *Alert* and had certainly had an interest in the coal trade. For some years, he had been the lessee of Polruan Town Quay, receiving fees from any merchandise

Part of Christopher's will showing Jane's firm signature as executor unloaded and rented cellars on the Quay for storing coal. His will was proved in April 1870 and his effects were valued at £2000.

The Family Board

Jane was now 58. She and Christopher had been married for 39 years and had worked in partnership for most of that time. Around her after Christopher's funeral were their sons and daughters. They were all adult, most of them married and well settled in their lives.

William Salt Slade, her eldest son, aged 35 had been apprenticed to his father at the age of fourteen and had worked with him for almost twenty years on all the Slade-built ships and was the yard's chief shipwright. He lived in East Street close to the main yard below. He had married Susan Ann Rowe and they already had a large family, eight children including twin sons.

Next in age was Thomas, 33, said to be Jane's favourite. He was married to Mary Ada Tadd, daughter of Peter Tadd who had commissioned ships from Slades yard. They had three sons and Mary Ada was expecting her fourth child. Thomas had been a mariner since he was fifteen and was now a qualified master mariner, licensed to 'sail across the world to any port in charge of schooners'. He was ashore at this time working with his brothers on the new ship. Then came John, 31. He had also been apprenticed as a shipwright from the age of sixteen and worked alongside his older brother. He was married to Ann Beer Hanson from Fowey. They lived in Fore Street with their son and daughter.

Christopher junior, 28, had started as a shipwright but was now a customs officer in Fowey. He had married Elizabeth Crapp Bate, the daughter of the Fowey postmaster and shipbroker. They had two sons, John Bate and Christopher. Susan was Jane's eldest daughter, aged 24. Christopher had lived to see her married to Peter Tadd, also a Customs Officer. This was the second Slade marriage with this significant ship owning family in Polruan. Philip Salt Slade, 21, the fifth son was also a shipwright, now fully trained and Jane's youngest daughter was Elizabeth, 18 and still living at home. Jane's last child was now ready to start his chosen career, Albert at 16 years old was committed to joining Thomas at sea.

Still at home was Samuel, aged 22. He had not been able to follow his brothers into a career in shipbuilding or at sea. An accident in the sawpit at the shipyard caused him to lose the use of his hand and possibly his arm. Family legend has it that his arm had been broken and was badly set by an incompetent and drunken local surgeon. With such a disability, Samuel was effectively barred from the family's traditional occupations as shipwright or mariner. For this reason he had been the only one of their children singled out for special bequest of £50 in Christopher's will. However, the accident had in some ways been beneficial. Samuel was now working in the office of William Wreford in Fowey as a solicitor's clerk. Wreford was an important man in the area being also the Customs Collector for the Port of Fowey. Having a son with legal and business training was a significant asset to the family business.

Jane's Decision

What of the business left by Christopher? Surely, Jane should take the opportunity to retire and enjoy her twelve grandchildren and let her adult sons run the shipbuilding, the inn and other interests? The answers were probably obvious to anyone who knew her. Jane placed herself firmly at the head of the whole enterprise as chairman of the firm. She would continue to run the Russell Inn, but would now also manage the rest of the business as well. William would continue as head shipwright at the yard assisted by John and Philip. From now the business was to be in her name: Mrs Jane Slade and Sons was the name by which they became known.

There was immediate pressing business for the firm; potential customers needed to be reassured that nothing had changed as the firm had to continue to attract both repair work and new commissions. There was the family-built ship, Jane's namesake to be finished. Thomas and Albert continued to work with their brothers to get the ship ready for sea.

1870 - an Eventful Year

Before the launch of their ship, there was another local launch. On 7th May 1870, the *Royal Cornwall Gazette* reported: A *very successful launch of a fine clipper schooner was effected at Brazen Island Yard, by Messrs. Slade, on Tuesday. She is to be classed A1, 8 years at Lloyds, her dimensions are 102 1/2 ft long, breadth 24 1/2 ft and tonnage 184 and is expected to carry 300 tons. The vessel is called 'The Highland Lass' and is intended for the Mediterranean trade. She is the property of Mr. J. Richard, Schonnor, St Germans. The ceremony of christening was very effectively performed by Miss Mercy Barrett of Polruan.*

This article is as misleading as it is inaccurate. The ship was the Island Lass and the builders were not Slades but Butsons. It would have been quite an achievement for Slades to launch two large schooners in the same year. They may have been assisting in the latter stages, as the Slades were not the only local shipbuilders affected by family tragedy. A few weeks after Christopher's death and just two weeks before the launch of the Island Lass, Nicholas Butson had suffered a serious accident.

1870 23 April Royal Cornwall Gazette: POLRUAN. ACCIDENT.- *As Mr. Nicholas Butson, of the firm of N. and J. Butson, shipbuilders of Bodinnoc and Polruan, was engaged in working on a new vessel now completing at Brazen Island Yard, he by some means fell off the scaffolding and came with great force to the ground, sustaining a fracture of the skull and compression of the spine, besides other injuries. The unfortunate sufferer, who is under the care of Dr. Davies, of Fowey, lies in a precarious state.*

June 25th 1870 the *Jane Slade*

At last in June, Slades yard was ready to launch the ship that was to become their most well known ship. The *Royal Cornwall Gazette* Saturday June 25th 1870 announced the launch of a *prettily modelled schooner* from Slades yard at Polruan. John Keast in his *History of Fowey* gives an excellent description of the atmosphere: *It was a great day when a ship was to be launched. Flags and bunting were displayed and the cheers echoed across the harbour as the vessel glided down and slapped into the water......*

Jane Slade Registered 9 August 1870

ON:63691 Ton:159 Rig: Schooner Carvel Figure head: demi woman
Builder:Slade   Master:Thomas Slade

Shares	Name	Occupation	Residence
36	Jane Symons Slade	Shipbuilder	Polruan
1	John Hawken	Blacksmith	Polruan
1	Richard Clogg	Butcher	Polruan
2	John Edward Hocken	Sailmaker	Polruan
2	Elias Roskilly Tadd	Master mariner	Polruan
1	Fanny Stevens	Grocer	Polruan
1	Elizabeth Salt	Widow	Polruan
3	John Hicks	Yeoman	Lanteglos
2	Thomas Pearse	Yeoman	St Blazey
2	Thomas Mutton	Butcher	Lerrin
2	WilliamGeake	Gentleman	St Columb
6	William Luke	Merchant	Charlestown
2	Nehemiah Stevens	Gentleman	Liskeard
1	John Bawden	Cabinet Maker	St Austell
1	John Martin	Farmer	Fowey

This ship was built by the Slades, sailed by the Slades and majority-owned by the Slades. Unlike other Polruan ships, it was to be owned and managed by her builders. Her figurehead was a model of Jane herself. Great care had been taken with the carving of this figurehead. Jane was depicted in a very business-like collar and tie, befitting a woman of business, but with an elegant hat with a large white feather and holding a bunch of flowers in her hand. Jane held over half of the shares in her new ship, giving her occupation as shipbuilder, the only female shipbuilder in Cornwall. The rest of the shareholders were a composite group of local commercial interests and small investors. The *Jane Slade* was to remain majority-owned by the Slade family until she was laid up in 1928.

Work would now start on the complete fitting out of the ship and her rigging ready for her first sea trials and then her maiden passage: *a proud woman Jane Symons Slade must have been when she looked over the quay wall and saw her trim namesake fitting out in Polruan Pool.* This was when the master took control of the ship from the builders. The master's task was to decide the best rigging and sail plan for performance.

This was a testing time for all. Thomas would be very busy checking sail plans and rigging with his friend the local sailmaker, John Edward Hocken, designing the best sail plan for speed. The *Jane Slade* had unusual rigging, with four topsails (usually two or three) and this may have been seen as successful. It was copied in 1872 in the sail plan of the schooner *Thetis*, launched from the building yard of Butson.

Thomas had his hands full, but it was also a time to enjoy the luxury of being at home. From the age of sixteen when he went to sea, home leave was normally a few snatched weeks between passages. For this part year, he could be at home with his wife, Mary Ada and their children. He would also be there for the birth of his fourth child due that summer. However, on August 27th, tragedy hit the family again. With her sister by her side, Mary Ada died in childbirth with her child. The death certificate gave the reason as exhaustion in childbirth. Thomas was now a widower with three children, Thomas Herbert aged nine, James aged four and Samuel aged two. Jane again took the lead role despite her own widowhood of a few months and increased responsibilities as head of the firm. The ship had to start repaying the investment and Thomas would have to sail with her. Jane took the three young children into her home. From here she would manage the various business interests and care for her grandchildren with the assistance of her daughter, Elizabeth and her niece from Pelynt, Elizabeth Cock. So at last, after what must have been a subdued family Christmas, on 30th December 1870, Jane's namesake the *Jane Slade* set sail on her maiden voyage with her two sons on board, Thomas as master and her youngest son, Albert as an ordinary seaman.

1871 Life Settles Down

Jane took up the new threads of her life, bringing up her grandchildren and running the Russell Inn and the yards. She gave her occupation in the 1871 Census as an innkeeper, but her range of activity was broader than this. Her name appears as the managing owner of the *Jane Slade*. As there were 64 shares held in a ship, it had become common for one of the shareholders, usually the majority shareholder, to take responsibility for the accounting. Jane was in charge of the books for the ship and together with the

The crew agreement 1870, showing Jane as the first managing owner of the Jane Slade

master could also help in managing cargoes, finding them and acting as broker when need be. The main function was to handle all payments and account to the other shareholders at the annual share-out, when the performance of the ship and her crew was translated into share payments. Jane, with her sons, also had to keep the yard running by attracting business to the yard, such as maintenance business and finding commissions for the new ships to be built. She also had to keep full control over the various financial dealings. Long lines of credit were a normal feature of business life and good bookkeeping was essential. The Russell Inn continued to be a central place for conducting business. Ship auctions were held there, the masters and local businessmen who met there would exchange much trade information. Public meetings of various kinds brought Polruan people together.

POLRUAN ANNUAL COURT *The annual court for this town took place on Monday, the meeting being held at Mrs Slade's, Russell Arms Inn. Capt. W. Smith presided, and the following were also present - Mr. S. Longmaid, town clerk, Capt. T. Tadd, Capt. M. Salt, Capt. J.S. Salt, Mr. J. Bennett, Mr. H. Cossentine, Capt. Joseph Moss, &tc., &tc. The court is a very ancient institution, and is annually held for the purpose of electing officers, letting dues, &tc. On the present occasion Mr. H. Cossentine's tender was accepted as lessee for the tolls of the town quay, for the present year, at the sum of £10 12s. 6d.*

Captain William Salt

Jane's father, who had been a significant partner in the development of the various businesses, was now an elderly man and in October 1871 at the age of 89 he died. He

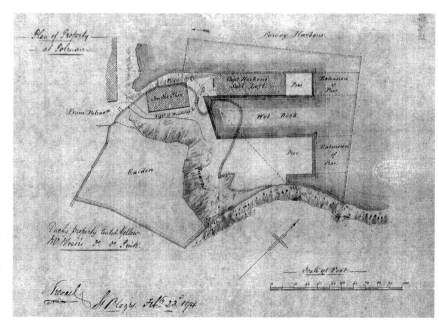

The Slade wet dock as surveyed 3 years later, in 1874, by Sylvanus Trevail (Cornwall County Record Office Ref:F/1/296/A)

had been living with his daughter, Susan Climo and his will drawn up in November 1867 is revealing. He had one son, John, and four daughters. Unlike Christopher's very even-handed will, William in his detailed bequests gave each individual different treatment.

To Jane, he left *all that Inn or Public House known by the name of The Russell Inn situate in Polruan to hold to her for and during the term of her natural life and from and after her death to Samuel Slade son of Christopher Slade.*

To his daughter Susan Dyer Climo *all that dwelling house and premises situate in Polruan, which I now reside in. To hold to her for and during her natural life and after her decease it is given to William Salt son of John Symonds Salt and his heirs. To Susan Dyer Climo all household furniture linen plate and glass except my writing desk and its contents which is bequeathed to Jane Symons Slade.* Here he gave all his business papers to Jane.

To his daughter Caroline, wife of Samuel Langmaid *the sum of five pounds to be paid to her at the expiration of six months after my decease and an annuity of two pounds during her life to be paid to her without any deduction by equal half yearly payments. The first to be paid six months after death. To be free from the control or interference of her present or any husband and to be payable by Jane Symons Slade out of proceeds arising from Russell Inn.*

After a few other smaller bequests, he distributed his shares in ships:

To *my said daughter Elizabeth Tippett two sixty fourth shares in the schooner 'Alert' and to my grandsons Thomas, John and Christopher Slade two sixty fourth shares each. To my daughter Jane Symons Slade two sixty fourth shares of and in the Brigantine 'Capella'.*

To his only son, John Symons Salt *all that freehold dwelling house, orchard and garden in which he now resides to hold him his heirs and assigns together with a leasehold cellar adjoining the premises he purchased of John Corners.*

Finally to Jane he left *my shipwrights yard (subject to the payment of certain monies advanced thereon by John Symons Salt), to hold to her during her natural life and after to my grandson William Salt Slade for his heirs for ever. Any other assets etc to Jane Symons Slade.*

It is clear from this will that William had a high regard for his daughter's business ability, leaving her all his business dealings and, despite the existence of a son, making Jane the executor of his will. The will had been drawn up some years before, at a time when women, especially their property and income, were a part of their husbands' belongings; the Married Women's Property Act did not become law until 1870. It also shows the extent of Jane's independence. When this will was drawn up, Christopher was still alive, yet Jane's father did not feel the need to suggest that her substantial inheritance should be free from the control or interference of her present or any husband.

Jane paid off the mortgage of £150 to her brother and so had complete ownership of the third yard and the Russell Inn. Slades continued in the business of repairing and building fine ships from their various yards. Following the launch of the *Jane Slade* in 1870, the next launch was in 1872, the *Snowflake*, built for Captain Samuel Tadd.

May 11 POLRUAN. SHIP LAUNCH- On Tuesday there was successfully launched from the ship-building yard of Messrs Slade and Sons, Polruan-by-Fowey, a beautifully modelled schooner. She is to be commanded by Captain Samuel Tadd, of Polruan; is intended for the foreign trade; is of about 290 tons burthen, and classed 10 years A.1, at Lloyds. Miss Parkyn, of Lerrin, christened the vessel The Snow Flake.(sic)

Snowflake Registered 25 June 1872

O N:63968 Ton:154 Rig Schooner Square stern carvel demi woman figurehead
Dim:L 98.8/B 22.7/D 12.1 Builder: Slade Master:Samuel Tadd

Shares	Name	Occupation	Place
14	Frank Parkyn	Merchant	St Veep, Lerrin
21	Samuel Tadd	Master mariner	Polruan
6	Jane Slade	Shipbuilder	Polruan
4	Thos Pearce	Yeoman	St Blazey
2	John Henry Hocken	Rtd Mster mariner	Polruan
2	John Edward Hocken	Sailmaker	Polruan
2	John Bawden	Upholsterer	St Austell
2	William M Scantlebury	Draper	St Veep, Lerrin
2	William Hy. Polybank	Gentleman	Stoke, Devonport
2	John Olford	Merchant	Lostwithiel
2	Nehemiah Stephens	Gentleman	Liskeard
2	John Hawken	Blacksmith	Polruan
1	Wm Ede	Gentleman	Polruan
1	Wm Henry Hony	Banker	Lostwithiel
1	Fanny Stephens	Grocer	Polruan

These ships were a special part of the local community's life. Captain Martin Tadd writing in *Sea Breezes* in 1955 recalled a launch as *a red letter day. On these occasions, farmers came in from the country to swell the crowd and a 'foo foo' or scratch band played a short ditty well known at the time as she moved down the slipway.*

There she goes to wallop the cat.

There she goes to never come back

The second line refers to the hope that the ship need not return for repair or modification to the shipyard or launching way.

The *Snowflake* was lost in 1882 while on a voyage from Goole to Plymouth with a cargo of coals; her master Samuel Tadd and his men were all lost. That was in the future, for now with another ship built and launched, the firm of Mrs Jane Slade and Sons was well established and the business was in safe and very capable hands.

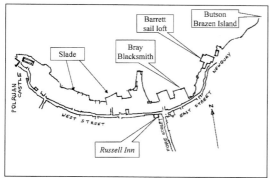

Occupiers of Polruan Yards c1860

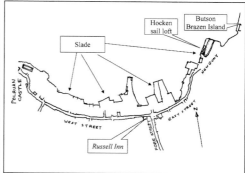

Occupiers of Polruan Yards c1868

The Jane Slade post 1903. Her master 1903-1910 was John Andrews of Liverpool (Mr and Mrs M Horton)

4
Thomas and the *Jane Slade*

..,.and here stretched the calm and solitary sea, the love of which had run in his blood even before birth. The ship was alive, sweeping her way over the surface of the water like a carefree gull, with Plyn a dark line far astern on the horizon

When Thomas left the harbour of Fowey on 30th December 1870, it must have been with some deeply mixed feelings. He had command of a new ship and had been involved in every aspect of her design and building. His crew included his brother Albert and he had brought his previous mate with him, William Boley. Compared to his last ship, the *Alert*, the *Jane Slade* was double the size at 159-tons and had a crew of six.

This was a significant moment in his career: a new ship and he was her first master. But he had lost his wife, his unborn child and his father in ten turbulent months. As they passed the harbour mouth out into the open sea, it would not have been surprising if he had briefly reviewed the events which had brought him here, standing on the deck of this ship that meant so much to him and his family.

As the second son of Christopher and Jane, his destiny was the sea. Seventeen years previously, he had joined his first ship at the age of fifteen. There had been no shortage of opportunities for passage on the many ships that frequented the harbour. Most of the male population of Polruan were deeply linked to the sea and just within his immediate family there were plenty of merchant captains.

A relation, Phillip Salt, was master of the *Alert*, a small coastal vessel of 93-tons. Her crew was usually five men, she worked her way round the southern coastal ports of England and Wales with cargoes of coal and clay and occasional passages to the Mediterranean. In May 1852 at the age of fifteen, Thomas was officially signed on as a boy, making up the crew to a total of six. His father, Christopher and grandfather, William Salt, knew this ship well; they had owned shares in her since her launch in 1842 from Butsons yard. Christopher may well have worked on her as a shipwright.

His first official journey lasted 1 year 7 months and 15 days, and he was back on board the next year back to the Mediterranean. Leaving Penzance on Nov 30th he sailed to the Mediterranean and then to Belfast arriving on July 22nd. He returned in time for Christmas at home on 20th Dec 1853. Now he had the taste for the sea, Thomas joined a variety of ships under different masters and in different conditions. After just two months ashore he got a berth on the *East Cornwall*, master William Smith, a close friend of his father, this time as an ordinary seaman and time aboard lasting fourteen months.

By May 1855, with barely two weeks at home, he was back to his first ship the *Alert* with his uncle. The following table gives an indication of the routes of these small coastal vessels:

Passages of Alert 1855

From	To	Arrival
Fowey	Swansea	1/7/55
Swansea	Pentewan	10/7/55
Pentewan	Burnt Island	2/8/55
Burnt Island	Newcastle	1/9/55
Newcastle	Newport	18/10/55
Fowey	Cardiff	19/11/55
Cardiff	Looe	4/12/55
Looe	Swansea	13/12/55
Swansea	Plymouth	-----------
Plymouth	Fowey	31/12/55

All of this was hard work in the extreme for the small crews, short passages between ports around the coast, backbreaking work hauling up the cargoes out of the hold by hand with a manual winch, reloading with the next cargo: always a race against time, tides and weather. A ship in harbour was not earning money for its owners and a fast turn round time to catch the best tide and wind was essential.

After the *Alert* with just a few days at home, he changed ships again, this time to the *Florence*, a barquentine. For his next ship he was moving up the career ladder as this time he got a berth as an able seaman on board the schooner *Ann & Elizabeth* until March 1858, after five months , when he transferred to the *Abel* promoted to bosun.

In all his passages, so far he had not had experience of an Atlantic crossing. He had mainly been in coastal waters, in what was called the Home Trade. However, in 1859 he signed on as able seaman on the 410-ton barque *Royal Adelaide*. This was a very different experience. She was a well-known passenger ship, sailing regularly from Fowey to New York and Canada with emigrants. He only served once with an emigrant ship, lasting eight months. It may not have been to his liking. Emigrant ships were not places of comfort. While the crew may have been well used to conditions on board ship, the passengers were more critical. A crowded ship with men, women and children, was not ideal. A contemporary, Richard Dingle, wrote a diary when he and his family emigrated from Polruan on the *Royal Adelaide* and complained bitterly about the overcrowding, the food and the attitude of the crew. Thomas did not stay long with the ship; on his return he had a better opportunity.

He signed on for his first passage as. mate on board the *Thomas Aylan*. She was brand new, launched by Butson in May 1860. She was Butsons largest ship to date, a schooner of 123-tons. He was aboard the *Thomas Aylan* for just four months and after this he did not return to sea for a year. Thomas had been moving steadily towards becoming a master. What he needed was an owner who was prepared to give him control of his own ship and the opportunity soon came. However, events in 1861 became a little crowded.

1861 the Sale of *Alert*

On 9th August 1861, there was an announcement in the *Royal Cornwall Gazette* advertising the sale by auction of the *Alert*: *auction to be held at Russell Inn, apply C Slade*. Christopher became the managing agent of the re-registered ship and despite only having had officially just four months experience as mate, he appointed his 24 year old son as her master. However, before Thomas could take command of his first ship, he had other matters to attend to. He was getting married and there was no time for the usual banns to be called.

A few weeks later on 1st September at Lanteglos Parish Church, Thomas (giving his occupation as master mariner) married Mary Ada Tadd, the daughter of John Tadd, master mariner from Polruan. They were married by licence and in October, Thomas sailed out of port to Gloucester, Plymouth and Par. He did not travel far from home as Mary was expecting their first child and two months after their wedding, their son, Thomas Herbert, was born on 8th November 1861.

Thomas' in-laws, the Tadds, were a Methodist family who had many links with the Slades. While Thomas and Mary were married in the Anglican Parish Church their son was baptised in the Methodist chapel in December 1861. Behind these bare facts of early appointment as master, marriage-by-licence, early births and different churches, the family discussions can only be imagined! Although in any seaport of that time, it is unlikely to have been an unusual event. Christopher and Jane could hardly comment.

In 1863 the crew records of the *Alert* show an apparent demotion for Thomas to bosun with William Bunclarke, 52, as master. The fact of the matter was that Thomas was not qualified to take the ship out of coastal waters. As Thomas did not yet have a Master's Certificate, he could not officially be master for a foreign passage. The solution often adopted was to take on a man with the necessary certificate to become the nominal master.

This does however highlight Thomas' need to get a certificate. These had become compulsory from 1850. In order to continue his career, especially, if he wished to extend the trades in which he dealt, such as the transatlantic trades in salt cod and fruit, he needed to achieve his Certificate of Competency. This required Thomas to enrol in a School of Navigation and sit the Board of Trade examinations. This may not have been quite such a large task. His early schooling in Polruan had not been as rustic as might be assumed. A previous schoolmistress, Mrs. Mitchell, was complimented for teaching three generations *reading, writing and arithmetic, among who are many masters of vessels, who owe their nautical arithmetic to her*. A good grounding in these matters had been essential for any boy wanting to go to sea and become a master mariner.

He enrolled in the Plymouth School of Navigation, Arts and Science in Gascoyne Place. The *Western Daily Mercury* quoted the fees as from 6d to 6s. In 1866 Thomas sat the examination in Plymouth and received certificate no 83310.

Now a fully qualified master mariner, Thomas went back on board the *Alert* again. A typical journey in the coastal trade in 1867 was to carry coal, china clay and ironstone. He kept his book on navigation beside him, with its sections on Decimal Arithmetic, Practical Geometry, Trigonometry, and Geography. The most used pages were the Map of the World and the Mariners Compass. In the flyleaf there are his jottings of dates and various calculations.

Alert   Passages Jan to June 1867

From	To	Cargo
Runcorn 1st January	Totnes 20th February	Coal
Totnes 7th March	Neath 24th March	Ironstone
Neath 31st March	Fowey 4th April	Coal
Fowey 18th April	Cardiff 26th April	Ironstone
Cardiff 15th May	Par 20th May	Coal
Par 3rd June	Runcorn 6th June	China Clay
Runcorn 26th June	Waterford 30th June	Coal

Master of the *Jane Slade*

Then at last here he was in December 1870, a fully qualified and experienced master mariner, on board the *Jane Slade*. Her very first passage would show him her sailing ability and his first port of call was to be Cardiff.

In Cardiff he signed the papers for her first foreign going passages. Naming his mother, Jane, as the managing owner he left Cardiff on 30th December arriving in Palermo, Italy nineteen days later. Here he loaded a cargo (probably lemons or raisins) and left the Mediterranean bound for the Atlantic, arriving in New York in April 1871, his first transatlantic passage in his new ship. A contemporary etching of New York shows the seaport in South Street. Where now there is a constant stream of yellow cabs and coaches filled with tourists, then the narrow cobbled hard between the harbour edge and the buildings were filled with horse drawn wagons and men, loading and unloading the ships. Chinese immigrants with their distinctive coolie hats, managers and merchants with their tall hats. The noise must have been tremendous.

Then he sailed back to Dunkirk and then finally home to Fowey in June 1871. However, not for long - two weeks later he left for Leghorn (Livorno, Italy) Hamburg and South Shields. For each passage, there was the paperwork to handle. In addition to the paperwork for the cargoes, there was the documentation for the authorities. In each port, the master had to report to the British Consul and lodge the ship's papers that showed the men on board. These were released before departure. Sometimes not all the documents were properly completed as in 1872 in South Shields.

Sir,

It is lately that I have joined a foreign going ship as master and I did not know it was required to enter Daniel Burgess in the official log book and if you will be kind to look over it this time I will be more careful in the future.

I am yours
Truly
Thos Slade, Master 'Jane Slade'

Daniel Burgess had left the ship at Hamburg on 11th Jan 1872. It is of interest to note the excuse from Thomas, rather surprising for a master of his experience.

The Proposal

One year later in 1873, at Hamburg, Thomas sat alone in his cabin writing an important letter. Until now, most of his letter writing had been confined to short battles with officialdom. This one was different and much depended on how it was received. He had waited until his brother had gone ashore. While in Fowey, Thomas had met Ann Hoal Bate, daughter of the Fowey Postmaster and shipbroker, John Bate. They were related through marriage, Ann's sister Elizabeth had married his brother, Christopher, in 1866.

Hamburg Thursday 23rd 1873
Dear Miss Bate,

My brother Samuel is just gone on shore for a little while this evening and I thought whilst he was out of the way I would pen you a few lines which I hope you will not think me intruding for so doing. I suppose you and your own people have heard by my brother Christopher or his wife of our safe arrival here. It looked rather gloomy the morning we came away to sail out of Port, but after we got out and proceeded up Channel it begun to moderate away and all the way we had a most splendid passage here, arrived on Saturday morning five o'clock all well. What do you think of me writing you to send me a few lines in return and we should still keep the correspondance up with each other. Of course you know how I am situated and I should like to have another partner in the course of a little time as I feel it is my duty to have one. I can truthfully say ever since I have been left single I never felt like I did the very first evening I saw you whilst home and that was at the Town Hall workmans tea when my Brother and myself spoke to you. There was a - something I felt within and said if ever I got married again I would like you to be the one.

Please excuse me for being so plain but my feelings will not allow me to be otherwise. And now of cours their is the second one to sanction this and that is yourself which I hope and trust will give me every satisfaction. When you get this and have carefully considered the matter over I should like for you to hand it over to your Father and Mother for them to pass their opinion on it as I should like to have all your comments on the matter and if it is pleasing for the one above to spare our lives I dont think we should have any cause to regret it. I kindly ask and intreat you after you have read it over and shown it to your Father and Mother you will just pen me a few lines which I hope to receive in due couse and *everything satisfactory on all sides. Should you favour my suit I will try all in my power to make you happy. I should like to have an answer as early as possible. Address to the care of Mr Daniel Milbery Ship Broker Hamburg.*

I am
Yours very Truly
Thomas Slade

He sent the letter with hope. It can only be imagined just how many discarded drafts were left on the cabin floor. The effort was rewarded and Miss Hoal accepted his offer. There is no record of her reply, but they were eventually married two and half years later.

More Officialdom

He was next in New York in 1874 and the ship's papers have two items written by Thomas on the same topic. The first is written into the ship's log:

New York 13 June 1874
Ernst Landelius deserted taking his effects. Ship being ready for sea and sailing after Consul's office open was unable to report desertion to him.
Signed: Thomas Slade, Master and John Hendy, mate

The second is copy of a letter written to the officials and attached to the Crew Agreement:

Glasgow 11 Nov 1874
To the Superintendent of Mercantile Marine Office

Sir,
Ernst Landelius, O S, on board the schooner Jane Slade deserted at New York and after consular hours
and ship being ready for sea had no opportunity of reporting such to the consul. Joseph Dooley was
shipped in his place.
I am, sir
Your obedient servant
Thomas Slade

Desertions were not unusual, sailors would jump ship to gain entry into another country. Landelius was Swedish and had been on board the *Jane Slade* for a previous visit to New York. New York must have seemed a promising city. However a desertion was bound to cause the master to get involved in awkward and time-consuming meetings with officials, these could delay the ship's sailing. It was probably (or intentionally) convenient that Landelius abandoned the ship at a time when Thomas was unable to contact the authorities.

Marriage

After his transatlantic crossings, Thomas was finally able to marry Ann. This was a very different wedding from his first. Ann's father was a significant figure in Fowey and plenty of time could be taken to arrange a suitable ceremony. On 29th July, 1875 they were married in St Fimbarrus Church, Fowey, he was 38 and she was 28. Ann had a new family of three sons, Thomas Herbert aged thirteen, James, nine and Samuel, seven. However, it seems as if Thomas Herbert remained with his grandmother, Jane. Almost fourteen, he would soon be a sea with his father. Thomas and Ann did not spend long together, in August Thomas was back on board the *Jane Slade* leaving Ann in her new home on Esplanade Terrace in Fowey. Over the next few years Ann and Thomas would have more sons, George, Alfred, and Frederick, but as yet no daughters. To help with domestic matters the household was completed with a servant, Rebecca Collings.

Cargoes and Crews

From 1876 there was a change in the cargoes carried by the *Jane Slade*. In December 1873, Thomas had sailed into Bristol. There he had arrived with another Fowey registered ship the *Gem* (with a Polruan master, W Smith), already unloading her cargo of fruit. Bristol harbour had several ships unloading fruit from St Michaels in the Azores. The ships had all arrived in January when the cargoes of oranges from the Azores fetched high prices in the winter market. That same year Thomas took on board as crew, two men from the *Gem*, John Hendy and John Martin who had experience in the fruit

trade. Their experience would be valuable. In 1876, the *Jane Slade* and her crew undertook her first passage to the Azores. While she had been previously been trading in fruit from the Mediterranean, this was the beginning of her regular trade to and from the Azores and then to the West Indies. It is in this trade that she won her reputation for speed. Basil Lubbock, the historian, credits her with the record-breaking journey from St Michaels to Bristol. Successful fruiters had to be small (to get into small harbours and to carry light but very perishable loads) and fast (speed was vital in the race to get back with a cargo of ripening fruit and to get the best market prices).

When they arrived at St Michaels in the Azores, they loaded 2184 packages of oranges and 4 packages of pineapples, then set sail for England, arriving in Hull on 22nd December 1876. She had taken just 14 days in winter weather, up the Channel and along the east coast to the Humber Estuary, hurrying to get the fruit back in time for the best prices, two days before Christmas.

While carrying fruit was lucrative, it meant braving the worst winds and weather. On 28th February 1885, they arrived in London from St Michaels (passage 14 days) and docked at Nicholsons Wharf with 1708 packages oranges, 92 packages tangerines, 154 packages pineapples, 9 packages potatoes, 2 packages pumpkins. This was a typical fruit cargo and from time to time, notably when discharging in Bristol, there was one extra package of fruit for Mrs J Slade.

The fruit trade may have been lucrative, it does not appear to have been passed onto the crew. The crew had all signed on at Bristol on Dec 31st 1884. In thirty-one years wages had not changed very much since Thomas had first gone to sea in 1853 on board the *Alert*. For two months' work, the crew's wages (after deductions) on discharge from this passage, were:

Crew Wages in February 1885

Name	Age	Birthplace		
Philip Read	38	Plymouth	Mate	£5. 7s 6d
James Sidney Slade	19	Polruan	Bosun	£3 10s 9d
Percy Hill	19	Barbados	Cook	£3 13s 6d
James Glen	25	Cardross	AB	£2 14s 11d
Peter Jensson	25	Denmark	AB	£2 0s 0d
James Malcolmson	40	Lerwick	AB	£2 0s 0d

Ships went where there were cargoes and in 1880 he had his longest passage across the Atlantic to the River Plate, Brazil to pick up a cargo of horns. On his return it seems to have slipped his mind that he had several years experience in the Coastal Trade.

I, Thomas Slade of Fowey in the County of Cornwall. master of the 'Jane Slade' of Fowey offl. no. 63961 do hereby solemnly declare that I arrived in Liverpool from the Brazils in the said vessel, and at Liverpool I landed a cargo of coals for Plymouth, and that on my arrival at Plymouth I omitted, through want of experience in the Coasting trade to deliver up the Home Trade agreement as required by law.
I further declare that I am now bound on a voyage to Leghorn in the said vessel and now wish to have the receipt C.C. and I also declare that there being no magistrate here on the death of Mr Treffry, that

I have been unable to get this declaration taken according to law.
Thomas Slade

Declared before me this 31st July 1880
Ezra Harris, Collector of Customs
No resident magistrate

Another short note in the ship's papers again shows the constant pressure on the masters to keep their ships moving.

Bristol 27th Febry 1883

Sir,
You having called my attention to the engagement of John Toben having been made at South Shields on 26th December last other that before the Shipping Master I beg to say one of the men proved to be a deserter an the vessel being ready for sea, and that day being a Bank Holiday I could not go to the Shipping Office and did not feel justified in the interest of my owners of losing an opportunity of a fair start down Channel, so I took the first man that offered and entered the occurrence in my Official log Book - which I trust you will consider sufficient
I am, sir,
Your obedient servant
Thomas Slade Maser
of sch r 'Jane Slade' of Fowey.

As seen in his letter to Ann in 1873 the Jane Slade carried other members of the family, in that instance, his brother Samuel was with Thomas, presumably on business with the broker in Hamburg. Samuel was also on board in March 1885 for a much longer passage from Fowey to Cat Island in Bahamas. This time Samuel is listed as officially part of the crew and it is described as his first ship. His presence increased the normal complement of six by one. The men on board included Thomas' two eldest sons, Thomas Herbert, as mate and James Sidney, as bosun.

Arrived at Cat Island 3rd May 1885 and sailed for London 10th June 1885. No British Authorities there
Thomas Slade Master, London.

They arrived in London on Tuesday evening, July 14th 1885 at London and on the same day the Undine of Fowey arrived also from Cat Island. There must have been something of race between these two ships, as they battled across the Atlantic. The Undine was the last ship launched by Butsons in 1875 and Thomas frequently encountered her and other Polruan vessels, engaged in the same trades.

1	*Thomas Slade* Master to sign first	1837	Cornwall		Same Ship	Continued		83310	
2	*Thomas. H. Slade*	1861	do	1887	Jane Slade Fowey	3/9/87	Fowey	Mate c122433 Aronie	
3	*William C Slade*	1860	do	1887	do	3/9/87	Fowey	Bosun	aronie
4	*George Friend*	1866	Kent	1887	Clyde Faversham	3/9/87	Fowey	Cook Seaman	aronie
5	*W H Marten*	1867	Rainham 20852	1887	Jane Slade Fowey	3/9/87	Fowey	AB	aronie
6	*William Johnson*	1865	London	1887	Maria Hayle	3/9/87	Fowey	AB	aronie
7	*Samuel Todd*	1869	Cornwall	1887	Jane Slade Fowey	3/9/87	Fowey	OS	aronie

The cargo, Thomas and his men unloaded, comprised of 3390 dozen pineapples. How many they started with is not recorded. Each day the cargo had to be inspected while at sea and any bad fruit thrown away. Pineapples cannot have been the most popular cargo to handle. The crew's wages, again after any deductions, for the period from 21st March, when they left Fowey, until 14th July 1885 when they unloaded in London were the following:

Crew Wages in July 1885

Name	Age	Birthplace		
Thomas H Slade	24	Polruan	Mate	£17.3s 5d
James Sidney Slade	19	Polruan	Bosun	£11 19s 3d
John Sweet	43	Polruan	Cook	£4 11s 3d
James Malcolmson	40	Lerwick	AB	£8 3s
William Gibson	22	Southampton	AB	£7 4s 9d
Samuel Slade	38	Polruan	OS	£0 3s 10d
Mark Carne	16	Newquay	AB	£10 5s

The next year they arrived from Charlestown, West Indies with 360 hogsheads, 279 barrels of sugar, 25 barrels tamarinds, 10300 cocoanuts and 1 package of merchandise. The spelling is correct, the third item was cocoa not coconuts.

This time Thomas had on board his eighteen-year-old nephew, John Bate Slade, son of Christopher junior. During Thomas' time as master, the ship was to act as a training ship for many of the Slade family. These included two of his brothers, Albert and Samuel, three of his sons, Thomas Herbert, James Sidney and George Hewitt, and nephews, John Bate, Samuel Peter, Christopher and even an Ambrose Slade from Pelynt.

The ship worked constantly in all weathers, in and out of ports. A Fowey man, Sydney Samuel was fifteen when he signed onto a Fowey vessel in 1896. He recalled *the voyages were fraught with danger and discomfort – climbing aloft to put on or shorten sail, in calm weather or gale, cold and wet in the North Atlantic or hot and steamy in the tropics and then on arrival in port having to set to and discharge the cargo with shovels and baskets and a hand and dolly winch. Food was very poor – tough salt tack (beef), weevils in the hard biscuits and cockroaches in the stew! Water was often in short supply especially if the voyage was prolonged by bad weather.*

So when the *Jane Slade* arrived with a cargo of 2683 cases of lemons from Messina, Italy, it is worth considering what that meant to the small crew. Each case was loaded manually into the hold and then 2683 cases had to be unloaded in London in the winter, December 1888. This was repeated in each port they visited, in all weathers.

The days of fruit carrying were numbered, it was becoming harder to get the cargoes and increased competition from steam tonnage on ocean routes was pushing older sailing vessels into coastal trades. 1889 was her final passage to the West Indies. A list from 1889 shows the variety of cargoes as she came and went from Fowey. Sometimes the master acted as his own broker at other times local Fowey brokers are noted, including his brother-in-law, GH Bate.

Fowey Harbour Commission Cargo Records

Date		Broker
22nd Jan 1889	Came in ballast, took out general cargo to San Salvador	Bate
18th Aug 1889	Came in ballast, took clay out to Trieste	--------
9th Jan 1890	Came in for orders carrying valonia, went Bridgewater	--------
28th Feb 1890	Brought in coal, went to Par in ballast	Master
24th Mar 1890	Wind bound. Came in carrying clay, went out to Genoa	Master
21st July 1890	Came in for orders carrying valonia, went to Bristol	Master
4th Oct 1890	Came in carrying coal, took clay to Genoa	Bate
8th July 1891	Came in carrying coal, went out with clay to Leghorn	Master
14th Nov 1891	Came in for orders with oil, went to Goole	Master
2nd Jan 1892	Came in ballast, took clay to Leghorn	Hannan
20th July 1892	Came in carrying valonia, went to Bridgewater	Master
22nd Sept 1892	Came in with coal; went out with clay to Genoa	Hannan
18th Feb 1893	Came in carrying valonia; went to Bridgewater	Master

These now were the regular cargoes to be carried - valonia is a type of acorn from the Levant that was used in the tanning process. When in some instances the records note 'coming in for orders', this was when the master had picked up a cargo in anticipation of finding a market for it on return.

It was on her run to Genoa in 1891 that Thomas had to report a tragic incident to the Consul.

British Consulate Genoa
Jan 9 1891
I certify that the master has reported to me the death of Albert Pearson that his wages (if any are due) and his effects will be accounted for on the vessel's arrival in the United Kingdom. I further certify that I have sanctioned the engagement of Walter Cumme and Fred Claesson upon the terms mentioned in the written agreement that I have ascertained and am satisfied that they fully understand the said agreement and they have signed their name in my presence. Edmund Reader British Vice Consul

On arrival in Bristol he faced questioning from the Mercantile Marine Office; deaths were serious matters and required investigation.

Bristol June 21st 1891

I have enquired into the cause of death of Albert Pearson late O.S. It appears he went on shore at Genoa, after working hours on 14th Nov 90, without leave; about 8.30 pm. he told the B. S. who was also ashore, that he was going to return on board: to get on board he had to cross the Railway track. Instead of crossing at the proper place, he went down the line, thinking to make a short cut, he was knocked down by a passing train and terribly mangled, the poor fellow was perfectly sober having had only one penny glass of wine.

J A Atwood, superintendent

Now, in 1891, lucrative cargoes were getting harder to find for sailing vessels, steam was now more effective and could get to the smaller ports. The following year was Thomas' final passage as master of the *Jane Slade*. In 1892 Thomas Herbert, his eldest son, met him in Leghorn and took over as master. Thomas, by now aged 55, was considering a change. He had been at sea for 40 years.

The cargo from the Jane Slade unloaded at Bristol on monday February 26th 1883

JANE SLADE, of Fowey, Slade, ST. MICHAELS	
149 Tons *Chessell & Co*	
2233 flat boxes oranges	C. F. Ivens & Co
1 bskt do	do
54 pkgs pines	do
15 pkgs tangerines	do
8 pkgs bananas	do
4 pkgs pines	Budgett, James, & Branth
5 boxes oranges	T. Slade

5
The Last Ships

He would rise in the mornings keen and refreshed, eager to get to his work and be out in the open, and content at the prospect of a full day in front of him. This work too, once fancied as monotonous, was varied and absorbing, it was like a miracle to watch the gradual growth and shaping into a stately vessel from what had been loose timbers and rough planks

After the launch of the *Snowflake* in 1872, the yard of Mrs Jane Slade and Sons witnessed several more new ship launches. While Thomas and his young brother, Albert, remained at sea, Jane's other sons continued the work of the five shipyard sites in Polruan. Slades and Butsons were now the major shipbuilders on both sides of the harbour. William, John and Phillip Slade were fully occupied with the repair and maintenance business. William, as chief shipwright, signed the builder's certificates for the ships and answered any queries from the surveyors. However when it came to contracts, leases or any other similar matters it was Jane whose name was given. The records of the Town Trust refer regularly to Mrs Jane Slade and Sons, when they rented the cellars on the Quay or were involved in local maintenance of the fabric of the Quay. When Jane registered her shares in ships her occupation was given on most occasions as shipbuilder. She continued to actively invest in a variety of ships. She bought four shares in the *Kingaloch*, a Canadian built ship in September 1871, and was part owner of the *Alexandrina* in 1873. These may well have been ships that were adapted or altered in her yards.

In 1873 there was a family celebration when Jane's youngest daughter, Elizabeth Ann, aged 21 was married to John Edward Hocken at Lanteglos Church. John was the Polruan sailmaker and had worked alongside Richard Barrett the earlier Polruan sailmaker. The Hockens were significant investors in local ships and John was based in the sail loft beside Newquay dock and worked in close partnership with the Slade shipyard. Here in 1874 Sylvanus Trevail, a local surveyor (later to become one of Cornwall's most well-known architects) came to survey this part of the yard. In Trevail's precise drawing,(see page 40) Captain Hocken's sail loft, the smithy and the dock and the quays are all detailed. The shipbuilding continued with the launch in 1874 of the *Silver Spray*. Just four years after Christopher's death the newspaper report now referred to *the well-known yard of J Slade & Son*. The *Silver Spray* was built for Nathaniel Hocken. She was 169-tons net and classed A1 for 11 years by Lloyds Survey. She was felted and yellow metalled ready for voyages to warmer climates. This process of adding felt and copper was to protect her wood from the ravages of tropical worms. F & YM is always an indication that the ship was built for warmer waters. Jane had significant number of shares in this ship and unusually, her occupation here is not as shipbuilder but as widow.

Shipbuilding was slowing down in the port and indeed across all the small shipbuilding

yards in the West Country. The small craft based yards could not compete so well with the increasing sizes of iron ships powered by steam. Despite this, a new shipbuilding enterprise started on the opposite bank of the river. In Fowey, John Stephens had set up as a shipbuilder in Whitford Yard, today the site of the Royal Fowey Yacht Club. Here in this small base he launched the 195-ton barquentine, *Ocean Swell*. The story is told that he had materials left over from this and the building of a second smaller ship was considered. Here, space, the constant problem of Fowey-based shipbuilders raised its head. With one ship still being finished in Whitfords yard, Stephens' solution was to take space in a Polruan yard and so the well known *Little Beauty* was built. She was the first of his fleet of ships known as the Little Ships. She was built in one of Slades yards probably at Newquay dock, during a time when Slades had a gap in their new ship production. The Butson yard at Brazen Island was meanwhile fully occupied with *Undine*, which was to be their last ship.

In 1875 *Undine* was launched by Butson. This 174-ton brigantine signalled the end of shipbuilding for the Butson firm of shipbuilders, they now concentrated on repair work and left the Brazen Island site, moving their operation wholly to Bodinnick. Work for the yards had to come from any direction and Jane and her sons in June 1877 were making and repairing boats for the local Customs House. Later in the same year, they were noted as J Slade & Sons colour merchant(paint merchants) and then in 1878 Jane Slade & Sons boat builders.

The Last Ships

In May 1877 one of Polruan's most well known ships was launched. The 243-ton barquentine the *Koh-I-Noor*. She was built for William Smith, a retired master mariner of Polruan who owned 21 shares. The same William Smith who had written the letter defending his friend Christopher Slade in 1864. The *Koh-I-Noor* was large and had a lengthy list of shareholders, many of whom had just one or two shares, thus spreading the risk among local owners from a wide area around Polruan. Jane is on the list of initial owners along with her brother-in-law, John, owner of the Axe Inn at Pelynt and her son-in-law, John Edward Hocken.

While work continued at steady pace at the yards, there was still time for relaxation. The three brothers, William, Phillip and Samuel were in evidence at the Polruan Regatta, then as now a time for enjoyment, but due to an overabundance of similar regattas in the harbour the crowds were not in evidence.

1877 September 21 POLRUAN ANNUAL REGATTA.- The little town of Polruan, situated on the banks of the river Fowey, held its annual regatta on Tuesday, but although the weather was lovely, the prize list tempting, and the various events well contested throughout, little interest was manifested in the proceedings. This is probably to be accounted for by the fact that during the present year no less than five regattas have been held in the river, and the people of the district have thus had quite sufficient of this particular kind of amusement. The committee who carried out the sports, were Messrs. T.H. Woods (treasurer), S. Slade (secretary), P. Slade, P. Harvey, J. Ellery, J. Trewin, Searle, J. Scantlebury, (clerk

Polruan Castle, which would have given Jane a very good vantage point from which to view her ships (Christian du Maurier Browning)

The barquentine
Koh-i-nor
launched in 1877

of the course), Captain W. Smith (starter), and Messrs. Barry, R.N., and W.S. Slade (umpires). The band of the 3rd Cornwall Volunteers was present on board the committee boat, and played selections of music at intervals during the afternoon. The steamer Sir Francis Drake made an excursion from Plymouth, and a number of persons availed themselves of the opportunity of visiting Looe and Fowey, and of witnessing the beautiful scenery for which the coast of Cornwall is so famed.

Repair work continued, the siting of one of their yards so close to the main quay in Polruan was a handy location. Work could be undertaken while ships were moored up at the Quay, but activities on or near Polruan Quay, then as now attracted the curious.

1878 October 11 FATAL ACCIDENT AT POLRUAN.- Inquest on William Menear, a lad of 10 years who met his death through falling in the hold of the schooner Waterlily while the vessel was undergoing repairs alongside the Town Quay at Polruan. After the jury viewed the body, William Climo said he was a shipwright living in Polruan - on the 21st September about 3 pm he was at work on board Waterlily. He found deceased at the bottom of the ladder of fore hatchway but didn't see him fall. distance was 8 to 9 feet. Found him bleeding from his left ear. At once he carried him up the ladder and had the lad removed to his home. James John said he was working in the hold of the vessel on the day mentioned, heard a fall and looking around saw the lad at the bottom of the vessel. Dr. A.P. Davis, surgeon, Fowey, stated there was no external injury but a very tender spot over his left ear, also a deal of hemorrhage in the left ear. Considered the child had received an injury over a portion of the temporal bone and attributed death to fracture of the skull. Verdict - died from accidentally falling into the hold of a vessel.

The Last Great Ship

While repair work continued at the central yard, Slades' other site at Newquay, next to Brazen Island, was occupied with the building of their biggest ship to date, the largest ship that would be built in the Port of Fowey. Work on the ES Hocken had started in 1878, Slade and Sons were paid £712 8s 8d as a first payment on April 27th. By September 1878 the total of the first stage payment was £1280. By the time the ship was launched in 1879 she had cost £5,250 to build. The last payment to the shipbuilders was on April 15th 1879, the date of her official registration in Fowey Ships register.

In the financial ledgers of ES Hocken, Jane Slade of Polruan paid £40 for two shares, at £20 per share the ship was valued at £1680. The ES Hocken was to remain in Hocken ownership until 1912 and was a regular sight in the harbour. She was to be the final Slade ship. There was no demand for new large wooden sailing vessels, steam had won the day. John Stephens in his yard at Fowey had experienced severe financial difficulties, becoming insolvent and leaving a partly built ship in the yard. This ship was later finished and launched as the Zingari in 1880. Stephens gave up shipbuilding and concentrated on ship owning and brokerage. In the same year that Stephen's insolvency was announced, in September 1879 the Royal Cornwall Gazette remarked on the growing number of visits by yachting men, both steam and sail.

The ES Hocken, the largest ship ever built in the port of Fowey

The Pride of the Channel *in the Slades wet dock. Next door is Hockens sail loft - pre* 1897

Retirement

Jane was now aged 67 and although she was still very active - her name is mentioned in Polruan Town Trust minutes as renting a new cellar from them - she had finally decided to retire from some aspects of her varied business interests. Two years previously she had handed over the management of the Russell Inn to her son, Christopher junior.

Christopher was her fourth son and had, like several of his brothers, been apprenticed as a shipwright to the family business. In 1862 in the *West Briton* it was reported that on 21st Nov at the Tywardreath Petty Sessions:

Christopher Slade of Polruan and John Pearn of Fowey appeared to summons charged with rolling a lighted tar barrel through the streets of Fowey on 5th inst . The case was proved by P.C. Parkyn and defendents were fined 1s and costs each.

He was then aged 21 and at the end of his apprenticeship, the incident may have been part of the celebrations by both young men on finishing seven years apprenticeship. Shortly after this incident he joined the Customs Service in Fowey, taking his oath of office from the Collector of Customs, William Wreford, on 20th September 1864. The two events may not have been entirely unconnected! However he had sufficiently redeemed his respectability three years later when at the age of 25 he married Elizabeth, the daughter of John Bate, Postmaster of Fowey and shipbroker. He remained in the Customs Service for another ten years, first as an Outdoor Officer then with the title of Tidewaiter. This delightful title meant that he was tasked with boarding the ships as they arrived to check for contraband. He remained with the Customs service for twelve years, leaving the service in 1878 when he and his family moved into the Russell Inn.

It must have been a hard task for Jane to leave her home, she had been living there for forty-eight years. She moved to St Saviour's Terrace in Polruan. This was a time of change for other members of the family also. Jane's move had an impact on her fifth son, Samuel who was still living at home with his mother. The accidental damage to his hand in his teens had stopped him from following his brothers' occupations and he had worked with William Wreford, as a solicitor's gentleman (presumably as a clerk). This is the same William Wreford who was Collector of Customs. It did not seem to hamper his career, Samuel's signature appears on many family documents. He had became very involved with local social and town activities, signing the Polruan Manor Court Minutes from 1877 to 1881, appointed as bread weigher from 1878 to 1881. In 1881, age 33, his occupation was as accountant and he was by now a key figure in the financial matters of the family business. He was still single some time after his brothers and sisters had married and had continued to live with his mother at the Russell Inn. Perhaps nudged by his mother when she moved from the Inn, he decided finally to set up his own home. In 1881 at Lanteglos Parish Church he married Mercy Barrett, daughter of Richard Barrett, the sailmaker. On this important occasion Samuel gave his occupation as shipbuilder, reflecting his close involvement with the family business.

Jane could now relax, she had handed over the Russell Inn, William, John and Philip were running the yards with business advice from Samuel. In 1877 the third generation of Slades were starting at the yard. Jane's eldest son William had signed up his son,

Schooner Silver Spray *of Fowey. Captain Richard A Pearn, Master, off Fowey 1875* (*Mr Mrs W Abbott*)

another Christopher (not to be confused with his uncle Christopher junior or his late grandfather), as an apprentice to J Slade & Sons for seven years. Her two daughters, Susan Jane Tadd and Elizabeth Hocken were married with their own large families. However, in 1881, Jane gave her occupation as a ship's accountant. This formidable woman was still keeping a very close eye on the family's business interests.

A Time of Change

Jane had witnessed the last big ship launch from her yard; in the next few years the local community's investment was hit hard. In 1881 and 1882 there were several losses of Slade built ships. The *Juno* built by Christopher in 1864 was lost in collision in mid-channel 1881. Then in July 1882 the Tadds lost two of their ships the *Silver Stream* and *Snowflake*.

Overdue vessels of Fowey. Grave anxiety is felt for the safety of 2 vessels principally manned by Fowey men long overdue at their port of destination. 'Silver Stream', Capt. Tadd bound Cadiz - St. Johns, Newfoundland, and 'Hecla', Ellery Master, on similar voyage. Both vessels have been a great number of days over the average length of passage and as a number of other vessels have recently been lost on the same voyage, it is feared that unless intelligence is shortly forthcoming, these two vessels have also succumbed to the terrific gales experienced.

All hands were lost from the *Silver Stream* and the *Snowflake*, a tragedy for the Tadd family and for Polruan. In the same month the *Sparkling Wave* was abandoned after foundering north of the West Indies, fortunately the crew were saved. Jane saw four Slade-built ships lost in twelve months and the news for continuing viability of the remaining ships was not encouraging.

1882 16 June A revolution in the shipping trade seems to be in rapid progress. Everywhere we read of the formation of steam shipping companies, and it is evident that the ocean carrying trade of the future will be mainly performed by steam vessels....

One attempt to move business in a positive direction came when Samuel, together with other local investors, took over the now unoccupied site at Brazen Island. They set up a fish canning business named the Brazen Island Sardine Company to process the fish still found in the local waters.

For Jane, the last years gave time to spend with her many grandchildren. On 30th March 1885, the happy news was that Thomas and his wife, Ann, at last had a daughter, Dora, to join their family of five boys. This was special news for Jane; Thomas was said by many to be her favourite son. Jane was able to see her new granddaughter christened in August, before Thomas left the port once more on her namesake the *Jane Slade*. Thomas left on 29th September heading for St Michaels in the Azores to pick up a cargo of oranges for the London market. In his small crew were his two sons, Thomas and

James, plus his nephews, Samuel, Peter and John Bate, sons of Christopher junior. The ship was not due back in her home port until January. On 28th December 1885, this amazing woman, Jane Slade, died aged 72 years. It is just possible that Thomas was able to join his brothers and sisters to say goodbye.

A schooner alongside Butsons *yard at* Bodinnick; *the house is now known as* Ferryside

Jane and Christopher's grave at Lanteglos 'in early spring the first primroses nestle here' (Christian du Maurier Browning)

6
Samuel, the Man of Business

...next to the thorn hedge and the old elm tree. Their tombstone stands to-day. High above the waving grass, with long stems of ivy clustered about their names. Beneath the inscription are these words in faded lettering:
Sweet rest at last
In early spring the first primroses nestle here, and the scattered blossom falls from a forsaken orchard beside the lane

In the parish church dedicated to St Wyllow, the words on the headstones read of the loss of loved partners or parents and the tragic young deaths, many of them lost at sea. Over to one side, close to the wall just as it was described in 1930, is the headstone of Jane and Christopher Slade. Jane was buried here beside her husband on January 1st 1886. With most of her children and many of her grandchildren there, it would have been a large gathering. Thomas and the crew of the *Jane Slade* had arrived in Cardiff on 17th December. Thomas could leave his ship and head home. Even Albert, Jane's youngest son was able to leave his ship, *Lady Ernestine*.

The full inscription on the headstone reads:

In loving memory of
Christopher Slade
Who died February 29th 1870
Aged 60 years
Also of Jane Symons
His wife
Who died December 28th 1885
Aged 72 years
Sweet rest at last

Many of the local community who had known Jane for so many years predicted, as small communities will, that Slades yard would no longer survive without the woman whose drive and energy had been the main force of the business. Perhaps even her family wondered how matters would turn out.

Jane's Legacy

After the funeral, the brothers and sisters considered the situation. Jane had not left a will, but Christopher had left his estate in trust for his children and Jane's father had been clear about his bequests for William and Samuel. William Salt Slade, now inherited his maternal grandfather's yard in West Street and the ownership of the Russell Inn passed to Samuel. This still left the many business interests that Jane had built up over the years, shares in various ships and the coal business. What would happen to the rest of the family holdings such as the shipbuilding yards below East Street and the lease on the second yard in West Street? More importantly, who would continue in Jane's role as the main driving force of the family business?

With the great shipbuilding years behind them, new work was needed to keep the yards and the men employed. Someone had to find the orders and keep the books. William, the eldest at 51 was a skilled master craftsman, as was his brother, John. Their expertise was in eye and hand, a lifetime's knowledge of wooden ships, and of the men who worked with them in the yard. Their brother, Samuel, was the natural successor to Jane. He had the business experience and the contacts. His early training had been in a solicitor's office, where he learnt about that part of the law so vital to the Victorians, property and inheritance. He had been an advisor and witness to many wills and business contracts, handling numbers came naturally to Samuel. He was an active networker in today's terms, his collection of job titles and the number of committees of which he was a member was impressive. He had in his many years living with his mother Jane, worked alongside her in running the business, taking frequent trips with his brother, Thomas, to visit the foreign ports and meet with the brokers. The family could breathe a sigh of relief, Samuel would handle all the business matters, while they could continue their chosen specialisation at sea or in the yards.

The Russell Inn at the end of the 19th century when Christopher junior and his wife were in charge (St Austell Ales)

The Russell, owned now by Samuel, continued to be run by Christopher junior. Samuel and Christopher became partners in the coal business, utilising the coal cellars on the quay. William remained the head shipwright supported by John, aged 43, and they continued to run the main shipbuilding and repair business from the East Street yard. This included the rental of the dock at Newquay next to Brazen Island. There was also the small West Street yard, bequeathed to William by his grandfather; too small for major ship work it continued as a useful site for smaller jobs. This left the *Jane Slade* and the various shares in other ships. Jane on her death owned 14 shares, Samuel was to keep these, which together with the shares belonging to Thomas meant that the family remained as majority owners. Ship management remained with William Geake of St Columb. Once all arrangements had been made Thomas and his sons left for Cardiff on 3rd January to return to the *Jane Slade* and then set sail for the Azores, while Albert left to rejoin the *Lady Ernestine* which was due to leave on 27th January.

Shipbuilding and Repair

Slades yard had turned out some of its finest and largest ships during Jane's time as manager, a period that had been the peak time for schooner building. By the time of Jane's death the great days of schooner building were over. The last schooner to be built in the port of Fowey had been the 80-ton *Zingari* built by Albertus Dingle. The remaining sailing ships still needed considerable work done on them. While no business records remain for Slades yard, one measure of activity can be taken from the records that exist

John Slade, son of Jane Slade (John Beaven)

for the sailmaker, JE Hocken. His sail loft was next to the dock rented by Slades. His ledger from 1882 to 1901 lists the names of over 100 ships, regular visitors to the port in need of his services. While some repairs to the sails were minimal, many ships were in the dock at Newquay yard for major work. If the ship required significant and regular work to the sails, it also required constant repair and maintenance to every other part. These wooden ships were hard working ships with many livelihoods dependent on them. A ship in harbour was not earning money and margins were being squeezed by fierce competition. The Lloyds classifications were still needed for insurance and the yards were kept in occupation, working to satisfy the demands of owners and surveyors.

There were few other yards now operating in the area. The two Butson brothers, Nicholas and Joseph, had died by 1887. Their yard now concentrated on boat building and small repair work in Bodinnick. Without the access to Brazen Island (which by this time was taken over by Samuel's sardine factory) the Butson family had limited space in which to work on large ships. What work they did on anything large had to be achieved at low tide, beside the ferry crossing.

The Slade family had the advantage of both the central yard next to the coal wharf and quay in Polruan and Newquay dock. Here a ship could be brought into the wet dock, large wooden beams were fitted at the entrance to the dock and then sawdust (or ashes) was scattered onto the water. As the tide receded the sawdust (in plentiful supply in the yard) clung to the beams and plugged any gaps, giving an almost water tight space in which to continue the work.

While the days of large shipbuilding were over, new building did not suddenly cease even if it occasionally caused some problems, as reported in the *Royal Cornwall Gazette*: *1886 May 7 The launch of the new fishing boat 'May Queen' took place at the Messrs. Slades' building yard at Polruan on Sat afternoon. Some difficulty was experienced in getting her off, as the slip was too high at the lower end, and after sliding a short way she stuck fast and could not for some time be again started. She was subsequently towed off by the 'Gallant', steam tug. The boat, which is a good one, is to form a part of the Fowey fishing fleet.*

Any hope that this would lead to a new age of boat building was dampened by the following report the next year:

1887 Feb 11 Timber trade at Fowey during 1886 - The number of cargoes of wood imported with port of Fowey was 11....consumption of timber has been on the increase although at barely remunerative prices. Wood shipbuilding is entirely stopped and there has been a less number of fishing boats built than in former years owing to the bad markets for cured fish in Italy. Housebuilding in Fowey has had a spurt in the past year - two builders having run up ten houses for lodgings. Besides this there have been 2 private houses and one hotel erected.

At least there was some potential good news in the final sentence, the hotel mentioned was the Fowey Hotel which had been opened in 1882 to accommodate new visitors. The Fowey-Lostwithiel railway line, opened in 1883, was bringing an increasing number of tourists to Fowey. A journey by rail down the river from Lostwithiel not only being very beautiful in its own right, was for many infinitely preferable to the journey by sea. The railways were opening up access as never before and tourism was now becoming an important part of the local economy.

By 1890s recreative sailing and boating were well established. Yachting was now fashionable. In 1888 the Slades turned their hand to yachts, producing the *Foam*, a private yacht for Mr. Richard Foster. The news report gives an indication of the importance of such a commission to the local community, long starved of the excitement and work opportunities brought by the ship launches.

1888 May17 Sat. evening a yacht launched from the yard of Messrs. Slade and Sons, Polruan. She is built for Mr. Richard Foster of Lanwithen near Lostwithiel, is a beautiful model and is to be yawl rigged. Her dimensions are as follows; length of keel 40 ft, depth of hold 7 ft, beam 11 ft, length overall 49 ft., tonnage (builder's measurement) 22 ton. The yacht was christened the FOAM by Mr. Foster, this being the name of his old boat. The launch was quite a success, the craft gliding into the water in good style amid cheers of a large number of spectators, among whom were Mrs. R. Foster and Miss Foster, Major Foster, Captain Foster, Mr. Lewis Foster, Mr. and Mrs. H.D. Foster, Captain Jenkin R.N. and Mrs. Jenkin, Mrs. Richardson, Reverend Mr. Mugford and Mrs. Mugford, Mr. W. Pease junior and others. Mr. Foster entertained several friends and workmen (over 30 in number) at dinner at Ye Olde Ship Hotel, Fowey, after the launch. A first class spread was provided by Mr. and Mrs. J.M. Williams to which ample justice was done by those present. The usual loyal and other toasts were proposed and drunk, and a most pleasant evening was spent, hearty cheers being given for Mr. Foster on his leaving.

Ship Ownership

If work was confined to ship repair and maintenance, the Slade family in common with many other residents still held shares in several of the locally registered ships. Samuel held his mother's 14 shares in the *Jane Slade*. Thomas had built up his ownership to 19 over the years and was the majority shareowner. Samuel owned the majority of shares in the *Ontario*, a Prince Edward Island brigantine he had taken over from his father-in-law, Richard Barrett. He was also the managing owner and was the recipient of the bad news, later reported in the *Royal Cornwall Gazette*.

1889 May 2 A FOWEY SHIP SUNK.- The brigantine, 'Ontario', 128 tons register, Captain Willcocks, master, Mr. Slade, Polruan, owner, struck a sunken rock while rounding Start Point, on Thursday morning. She was in ballast bound for Fowey at the time. The Salcombe coastguards put off to her but found she had sunk about half-a-mile west of Prawle Point. They brought to Salcombe with them the captain, his wife, and child, and the crew of five.

The Family in 1891

By the time of the national census in 1891 the Slade family was well established in and around the harbour. Samuel lived in Cliff House, West Street, and gave his official position as shipbuilder and coal merchant. Here he lived with his wife, Mercy, and two nieces, Constance Barrett and Ann Barrett Stephens. Samuel had a range of other occupations to choose from: ship owner and manager, Clerk to the Parish Council, Clerk to the Schoolboard, Manager and Secretary of Brazen Island Sardine Co, and secretary of the Reading Room. His name was linked to almost every activity in Polruan, among the more colourful appointments were Ale Taster and Bread Weigher of Polruan Manor Court.

At 4 East Street, Polruan over the yard lived William Salt Slade, 56, shipbuilder. He had spent his whole working life in shipbuilding, his was the name on many of the surveys of Slade ships. He was most certainly the chief architect of the yard. He had one son working with him, probably still under apprenticeship, Alfred Colin aged 19, shipwright. But the third generation of Slades was beginning to move away to new opportunities elsewhere. William's son, another Christopher, after finishing his apprenticeship had moved to more exciting horizons in Chatham Dockyard. Here he remained with his son, another William, following in his footsteps and eventually his grandson, Keith Slade, retired in 1980 as the fifth generation shipwright of the Slade family.

John, aged 52, gave his occupation simply as shipwright. He and his wife Ann lived in Fore Street with their sons, Ernest aged 23, James aged 19 and Joseph aged 15. These three were all shipwrights or apprentice shipwrights at the yard. In West Street at the Russell Inn was Christopher junior, aged 49. He is described as *Licensed victualler, general merchant, publican and coal merchant*, the last was in partnership with Samuel. He and his wife Elizabeth had two sons, Samuel Peter and Archie, and one daughter, Annie.

Brazen Island
sardine canning
factory, previously
Butsons yard
(see p43)

Christopher at the Russell Inn was gaining quite a reputation as an expert selector of spirits. Curiously for a landlord, he was teetotal. A family story relates that when the salesmen came, rather than taste it he put some of the spirit in his hand and smelt the liquid, making his purchase on the smell alone.

Also with property in West Street, but not resident there, was Albert Slade, the youngest surviving child of Christopher and Jane. After becoming bosun on the *Jane Slade* he had gained his certificate of competency as a master at Plymouth in 1879. His first ship as master was the *Waterlily* in 1880, on her he sailed to the West Indies, the Gulf of Mexico, the River Plate and Brazil. By 1891 he had moved into the league of very large ships and world travel, with his ship the *Cogaburn* of Glasgow. A barque built in Dumbarton in 1882, it was 1068-tons and was owned by Caswell of Glasgow. He remained her master sailing to the South Pacific and west coast of South America, the East Indies, Burma, Mauritius and the Red Sea.

The other master mariner, Thomas, was still based in Fowey when he was not on board the *Jane Slade*. He was now aged 54 and his family was settled in a fine house on Esplanade overlooking the harbour. By 1891 Thomas' second family of three sons and a daughter, Dora, was joined by another son, Philip. Thomas' sons from his first marriage had left home. Thomas Herbert had gained his master's certificate and had left the *Jane Slade* in 1888 to take up his own ship, the *Gudrun*, sailing to South America. James Sidney had also served his apprenticeship aboard his father's ship, while Samuel Harold, his third son, had gone to Australia. Here he worked on the railways marrying Catherine Bertha Nilsson in St Phillips, Abbotsford, Victoria in 1890.

Phillip is the son of Jane and Christopher, about whom there is very little information. He was apprenticed to the yard and qualified as a shipwright but the only mention thereafter is a brief mention in the newspapers.

The Influential Family

By 1892 the family reached the peak of its influence in the port. In February 1892 Samuel was elected to represent his parish of Lanteglos on the board of the Fowey Harbour Commissioners. The post of harbourmaster was about to become vacant, so he rapidly alerted Thomas. Thomas Herbert, Thomas' son was now master of the *Pak Ling*, his first steamship, but whether by design or chance he was available to travel to meet his father at Livorno, Italy. As the *Jane Slade* came into Livorno, father and son changed places and in mid-April 1892 Thomas returned to Fowey. The position of harbourmaster was advertised one month later. Fifty applications were received and 15 were interviewed. Thomas was successful and just a few weeks later on June 25th he was made harbourmaster and Collector of Dues and provided with a cap and uniform. He received an annual salary of £60 and 5% of all dues collected. It all seemed so well arranged.

Elizabeth Ann, Jane Slade's youngest daughter who married John Edward Hocken, the sailmaker (A Samuels)

Tragically just one year after his return to live in Fowey in 1893, his wife Ann died aged 47. Their youngest child, Ruby, was just two years old. Ann was buried in Fowey cemetery and a grieving Thomas arranged a memorial to her on the wall in the church where they had been married. He was badly affected by this sudden loss, but the work of the harbour had to continue and this included the annual Fowey Regatta, an event of great significance in the local calendar.

Royal Cornwall Gazette Aug 24th 1893:
FOWEY ROYAL REGATTA Favoured with perfect summer weather, the annual royal regatta at Fowey on Wednesday, last week, was more than usually successful. Capt. Slade, Harbourmaster, kindly lent his schooner, 'Jane Slade', as committee vessel, his son, Capt. T. H. Slade, making the vessel most comfortable for committee and visitors. The committee were much indebted to Mr. Simon, a London gentleman who has a residence at Fowey, for generously augmenting the prize list, in addition to rendering assistance in making the arrangements. During the afternoon the Fowey Town Band played a programme of music on the committee boat....

Thomas had by now taken over as managing owner of the *Jane Slade* and retained a major shareholding. His eldest son, Thomas remained as master until 1894 when he left to become master of another Slade built ship, the ES *Hocken*, the largest ship built in Fowey harbour. The replacement master on the *Jane Slade* was his brother, James Sidney Slade for a brief period and then James Sidney moved on to the *Madagascar*. Then for some reason the ship was laid up for two years until 1896 when Adam Veale took command. Times had changed and the *Jane Slade* no longer made her passages across the Atlantic, she was occupied only in the shorter more frequent passages of the coastal trade. From now her main cargoes would be china clay and coal.

As harbourmaster, Thomas oversaw the main operation of the port. The silting up of the harbour had continued to cause problems for ships in gaining access. This had often been blamed on a combination of china clay deposits, and the habit of ships dumping their ballast into the harbour. Whatever the root cause, the need to clear it was vital, a silted harbour could not attract the ships from elsewhere for china clay that by now had become the main life line of work. Although as a footnote in the next extract shows, there were already tension with the increasing leisure pursuits in the harbour.

FOWEY NOTES. ...Our Harbour Commissioners seem to be setting seriously to work to deepen our harbour and to increase the facilities for vessels of large draught coming here for china clay. On Saturday a large 'dredge' arrived, which has previously been in use in connection with the harbour works at Mevagissey, so that we may see the work speedily begun. Some of us are still wondering whether Fowey is to be made a minor torpedo-boat station, and those who enjoy boating on the lovely 'Pont River' hope that this is one of the things that will not come to pass.

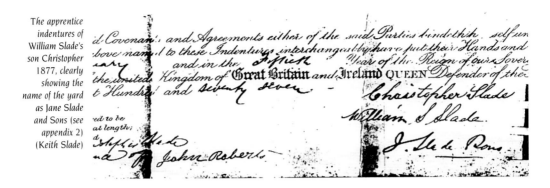

The apprentice indentures of William Slade's son Christopher 1877, clearly showing the name of the yard as Jane Slade and Sons (see appendix 2) (Keith Slade)

1897 Apr 15 NOTICE TO MARINERS, PILOTS, TUG MASTERS, BOATMEN, &C. FOWEY HARBOUR. DREDGING OPERATIONS *will* SHORTLY BE COMMENCED *in the above Harbour with the object of widening the present channel. All persons in charge of vessels or boats of any kind passing up or down the Harbour or River, are warned to take every care not to foul the Dredger's chains (which will be slacked down for them to pass, should it be necessary) and to pass on that side of the Dredger on which the Regulation Signals are hoisted, viz., 2 balls by day, and 2 bright lights by night.*

Steamers , when approaching the Dredger, must go dead slow, and stop their engines, if necessary.

Sailing vessels and steamers are requested not to go above the Buoy off Prime's Cellars without the permission of the Harbour-master, unless they are in charge of a Trinity Pilot.

Persons in charge of licensed pleasure boats, and others, are warned not to anchor in or about the channel, or to interfere with the free navigation of the river by the tugs towing hoppers, &c., connected with the Dredging, and are especially advised to keep clear of the wash of the tugs...

Samuel and Public Works

As a harbour commissioner, Samuel was also well involved in the work of the harbour. He had been as busy as ever in local matters in Polruan. Sanitation was a major concern; there were no proper drains and water still came from communal wells in Polruan, a problem that had been causing health concerns for many years. Typhoid had been reported in 1880 and was directly attributed to the appalling drainage. The arguments took many years to resolve, part of the problem being the charge to the rate for the Parish of Lanteglos of which Polruan was the major part, many of those who lived outside the village did not see it as something they should pay for. After all the arguments, at last it was agreed to set up Polruan's own waterworks, Samuel being a key player. In 1888 Samuel was part of the fund raising efforts to build a new mission church in Polruan to save the lengthy walk to St Wyllow. He donated a rose window in the west wall. In 1892 he underwrote the new street lighting for Polruan and in 1894 he opened the new girls' school. In 1896 he was responsible for organising the telephone connection between Polruan and Fowey, a technology that would be of real benefit to his business interests. Then finally in 1897 the Polruan waterworks were officially opened during the Queen's Jubilee celebrations.

Jul 1 CORNWALL AND THE JUBILEE Polruan - *The celebration was carried out in a hearty manner. Arches, festoons, and other decorations were liberally displayed. Under the leadership of Capt. Pelham Bullock a procession, consist of the committee, children, and adults, marched through the town singing. En route the Jubilee waterworks were opened by Mr. Samuel Slade. On St Saviour's-hill the children and the old people over 60 yrs of age had a free tea.*

Samuel was a very busy man and probably did not need the added problems of a court case. It was however as head of the family firm that he was to be involved in a case over a pile of stones, a case that was reported in the national newspapers. The plaintiff was a Polruan man, Captain John Hill.

The Times Newspaper, 19 June 1899
1899 Slade v Hill at Bodmin
Action brought before Mr Justice Phillimore and special jury, the case of Hill v Slade was heard on Saturday. Mr. Duke QC and Mr. Hawke appeared for the plaintiff; Mr. J. Alderson Foote, QC and Mr. W. T. Lawrance for the defendant. This was an action brought to recover damages for personal injuries in these circumstances. The plaintiff, a retired master mariner of 65, living at Polruan, rowed over in his boat to the town quay at Fowey on the morning of June 24 last year. He landed at the steps, but found that a quantity of granite building stone belonging to the defendant, who is a shipbuilder and merchant at Fowey, had been stacked above the mooring ring where he usually moored his boat, and he therefore moored the boat at another spot. He came back about midday, the tide having ebbed in the interval, and having unfastened his boat proceeded to lead it back by the mooring rope to the steps. When he got to the stack of stones he found it was impossible to go round the stones or in front of them, so he went on to the top of the stones. While he was so walking along a stone gave way and he fell over into the harbour, striking the side of his boat in his fall. He sustained various severe injuries, including a dislocated shoulder, which had incapacitated him from rowing or sailing his boat, or, in fact, from doing much work since. The plaintiff's case was that the defendant had no right to block up the public thoroughfare over the quay by placing stones there. On the other hand, the defendant's case was that the quay was a private one over which the plaintiff had no legal right of way. At the end of the evidence of for the plaintiff, it was submitted that there was no case to go to the jury. After argument, his Lordship upheld this view on various grounds, inter alia, that there was no evidence of any highway along the sea front of the quay. His Lordship therefore directed a verdict for the defendant, with costs, and certified for a special jury, but on the plaintiff's application execution was stayed for a month.

The End of the Century

Two of Samuel's brothers were not there to witness the publicity. The family had lost two significant figures. Albert, the youngest brother, had moved up the ladder in his chosen career and had taken charge of his largest ship. At 2077-tons the *Madagascar* of Glasgow was nearly twice the size of the *Cogaburn*, his previous ship. She was a barque, built in Port Glasgow in 1888 and her managing owner was James Boyd of Dumbarton. She sailed regularly to South and North America until 1899 when L*loyds List* posted the news:

New York July 27 Captain Albert Slade of barque Madagascar of Glasgow died at Long Island College Hospital July 25. He was only 45, he had progressed from small schooners (the Jane Slade was 159-tons) to one of the great sailing ships of the century.

Albert's early death came one year after the death of his eldest brother, the chief architect of the Slade ships. William Salt Slade had died at home in Polruan. William, who had worked on some of the largest ships built in the Port of Fowey had retired a few years before, leaving his brothers, John and Samuel to run the ship repair and boat building business. His legacy was his work on the ships and his signature on some of the ports finest vessels. It cannot have been a coincidence that the first ship attributed to Slade and Sons was built when William finished his apprenticeship and the last ship was launched just before his retirement. He was not a rich man, he left just £237 to his wife, Susan Ann. As the second generation of the Slade family of Polruan was passing on, so the third generation, Christopher and Jane's grandchildren were making their name at the yard as the new century began.

7
Ernie, Jim and Joe

By the autumn of 1911, orders came few and far between down to the yard. It seemed that no more schooners or barquentines were being built; owners were commanding iron and steel vessels from the up to date yards in the big ports, and the ever sounding hammer and saw was infrequently heard in Plyn these days

At the turn of the 20th century, one regular sound in Polruan, recalled in later years, was the sound of John Slade's hobnailed boots as he ran down to the yard from his home in Chapel Lane, at 6 am every working day. John, generally known as Jack, now had his three sons working with him at the yard, Joseph, Jim and Ernest. These were the men in the third generation who were learning the family business. They were learning their trade in difficult times as the world of the wooden sailing vessel was coming to a close. There was still plenty of work for the few operational local yards, a steady flow of wooden vessels needing maintenance and repair. The remaining sailing vessels were mostly working in the coastal trade with china clay, coal and other cargoes. With china clay still a significant export from Fowey and Par, Slades yard at Polruan and Tregaskes yard at Par were able to continue to attract business from both locally registered and visiting vessels. The two yards had the additional advantage of dedicated docks. Tregaskes had built his dry dock at Par in 1893. While not being a dry dock in its truest sense the dock at Newquay in Polruan was still able to keep Slades yard busy, such as a major refit of the *Lydia Cardell* in July 1901, commissioned by the Hocken family.

A vessel in Slades dock showing men working in the rigging (Author)

The men of Slades yard before 1900
Back row: Frederick Salt, Matthew Salt, Frederick Johns, Harry Braddon, Ned Dean, Tom Wyatt, Bert Luxton. Middle row: Charles Wakeham, Albert Pearn, Harry Rogers, Jack Welsh, Samuel Slade, John Slade, Nathaniel Toms Hunkin, Mark George, Joseph Slade. Front row: Ernest Slade, William Welsh, Benjamin Moss Tregaskes,

The Men in the Yard

Who were the men of the yard? A photograph taken in the early years of the century shows the two brothers, Samuel and John with their men. Samuel looking the part of the businessman, or 'quite the gentleman' as his niece, Agatha, was to say later. Some of the men are holding their tools of trade. Mr. Tregaskes was more than just a visitor to the yard, he was also the landlord for part of it, as he was the owner of Newquay Dock and the land around it.

Shipwrights in the Yard

Two of the men, Ernest and Joseph, were the sons of John Slade, their brother Jim was also working in the yard, but did not appear in the photograph. Skilled men were essential to the yard. The career of Herbert Luxton was an example. He was born in Mullion where his father was in the coastguard. When the family moved to Polruan they lived in West Street. At the age of 14 in 1902 he was apprenticed to Slades yard. Fourteen was the age at which most young men left school, but Herbert was fortunate in Polruan. 'Skipper' Widlake, the headmaster of the boys' school ran a night school so that they could continue their education. For Bert, there was a big advantage in being

apprenticed in Polruan. With home close by, the men could start work at an early hour, usually 6 am in the summer and 7 am in the winter then return home for breakfast.

After finishing his apprenticeship and getting his indentures returned with a note from Slades yard to say he had satisfactorily finished his term, he went to work at Hellars yard upriver, daily rowing himself up to Caffa Mill Pill. By 1911 he had left the area to go to Plymouth, attracted by the news that the dockyard was hiring men. The big dockyards could offer security and a pension, small local yards were unable to compete and lost skilled craftsmen on a regular basis.

The Slade Family

The Slade family of shipbuilders and master mariners were successful, hardworking and at the peak of their influence. Samuel was a Harbour Commissioner among many other titles, and if there was a cause or a committee he was deeply involved. Thomas was the Harbourmaster, Christopher junior ran the Russell Inn (now owned by Samuel) and John kept the yard running in partnership with Samuel. Although work was not what it had been, the Slade family was very comfortably placed. The 1910 Inland Revenue survey showed that the Slade family owned considerable property in Polruan, in addition to the Russell Inn. The only remains of their other interests in West Street, other than the Russell Inn, was a garden owned by Samuel. They no longer had any use for the two small West Street yards that by now were used for small boats.

Right: Thomas' daughter Dora and her first child Gladys, the author's mother. Far right: James Sidney Slade - 3rd master of the Jane Slade - son of Thomas' first marriage

Occupier	Owner	Description	Place
John Bate Slade	Samuel Slade	Russell Inn	Polruan
J Bate Slade	J Slade & Sons	House	---------
J Bate Slade	Self	Cellar, quay	---------
J Bate Slade	Town Trust	Cellar, quay	---------
Charlie Toms	S Slade	Sail loft	Newquay
Ernest Slade	J Slade & Sons	House, quay & town house	--------- East Street
Ernest Slade	Sam Slade	Garden	West Street
J Slade & Sons	Tregaske, Par	Shipyard	Newquay
J Slade & Sons	Selves	Shipyard	East Street
J Slade & Sons	Tregaske Smith	-----------	Newquay
Samuel Libby	C Slade	Land	Priors Field
Sam Tregaskes	Thomas Slade	House	Holly House

Retirement

In 1902 Christopher junior, at the age of 61 retired to a house in Fowey, handing over the Russell Inn to his son, John Bate Slade. John Bate had qualified as a master mariner, serving on the *Dunblane* a steam vessel and he had been master of the *Renfield* until 1900. His uncle, Samuel still owned the Inn and John Bate followed his father's footsteps and ran both the pub and the coal business, taking over the two coal cellars on the quay.

The *Jane Slade* was still in commission and was managed by Thomas. The shareholding in the family was unchanged; Thomas with his 19 shares and Samuel with 14 although

The Jane Slade moored beside Slades yard, showing the new motorised Polruan Ferry, built by Slades in about 1912

their brother, John, did buy two shares in 1903. She was occupied now solely in the Home Trade (around the coasts of Britain and Ireland and to the continental ports between Elbe and Brest in the coastal trade with coal and china clay). In 1905 she was refitted with three masts. This was a more economical rig, requiring fewer hands to manage the smaller sails. While her crew had previously been six plus the master, she now sailed with only four. She was still up to the high standards required of a Lloyds registration despite being over 30 years old. Her master was George Thomas of Port Isaac who had taken over from Adam Veale in November 1899.

Thomas, himself, was experiencing difficulties. He was aged 67 and his eldest son's wedding is the last time he is heard of as Harbour Master. Thomas Herbert married late in life at 41, marrying Rebecca Collings aged 36 in 1902. Rebecca had been the housekeeper who had brought up Thomas' youngest children after their mother's death. Just over one year after the wedding, in February 1904 the Harbour Commissioners, chaired by Sir Arthur Quiller Couch asked Thomas to resign 'due to ill health'. The Trinity House Pilots sub commissioners were not so diplomatic. Under Thomas's name they wrote just one word, 'insane'.

Bodmin Asylum

Thomas was admitted to the private wing of Bodmin Asylum. He was not the first Slade to be admitted. In September 1900, Samuel had been admitted as a private patient. The asylum took a wide range of patients, many today who would not be considered in

The Bristol Pilot Cutter Cornubia later renamed Hirta, built in 1911

need of institutional help. Depressive illness, Alzheimer's and elderly confusion, stress related breakdowns would all have been reasons for such hospitalisation. The asylum took over 800 men and women and up to 50 private patients who paid 21 shillings per week. Possibly Samuel had over-stretched himself with his wide business and charitable interests, suffering some type of crisis, but it was one from which he was able to recover. Nine months later he was discharged and he appears again in a variety of business records (in 1903 he was appointed Scavenger at Polruan Manor Court) and he was once again a Harbour Commissioner.

Thomas, like his brother before, was discharged as recovered in July 1904 and retired to Holly House, Fore Street, Polruan. Much of the evidence for his and Samuel's time in Bodmin come from the Visitors' Books. These are the minutes of the Board of Visitors set up to oversee the asylum and there are occasional errors on names, but confirmation that members of the family were having some kind of mental health problem is confirmed by the burial registers for Lanteglos by Fowey. In the next few years two further members of the family died in Bodmin Asylum. In January 1909, Thomas Herbert Slade, son of Thomas, died in Bodmin aged 47 just six years after his marriage. He had been the master of the *Ada Peard*, sailing her on passages to the West Indies and to the East Indies. By October 1906 he had retired at the early age of 45. Some time later he was in Bodmin. In December 1909 yet another member of the family died at the asylum. John, third son of Jane and Christopher died at Bodmin Asylum, aged 70.

The high incidence of visits to Bodmin Asylum in one family, three brothers and one of their sons, suggests that either they had a type of depressive illness (indicated by the recurring nature of the illness) or perhaps in the case of the older Slades that Bodmin was used as a home for the elderly when they could no longer care for themselves. Certainly, the parish registers for this time show a significant number of elderly Polruan people dying there.

Work in the Yard

With the death of his father, John, the main Slades yard was now in the hands of Ernest Congden Slade, known as Ernie, who took over as manager of Slade and sons. His father, John, had left his share of the yard and his two shares in *Jane Slade*, his estate was valued at £954 1s 2d. John had stipulated just as his father, Christopher, had before him, that his sons had the freedom to choose whether or not to continue in the business. If they did then Ernie was to be the manager and have the house above the yard in East Street on a token rent.

Ernie and his brothers inherited a struggling business, still part owned by Samuel. In 1907 they launched the *Lucy* B and in 1909 *Clarice*. These two were yachts, cutter rigged and 13 and 17-tons respectively. Repair work still came in, in 1909 they repaired the schooner *Olwen* for Captain Gregory, in what looks like a major refit. The bill heading shows the Slades as block makers as well as boat builders, and repairers. Previously there had been blockmakers and ropewalks across in Fowey, but now all these independent businesses had gone. Soon there would be no separate chandlers or sailmakers in Polruan. John Edward Hocken had retired to Fowey and so the Slades went into chandlery as well.

In 1910, the Hockens' *ES Hocken* came back to the yard that had built her to be repaired and to get her Lloyds Certificate renewed. This resulted in 1910 of a bill for the following items to Hockens on Oct 31st:

> *Survey class A1 for Lloyds of ES Hocken*
> *Slade & Sons Carpenter*   £185.3.10
> *Ship chandler*   £77.0.0
> *Smith*   £11.3.2

An invoice heading 1909, showing the unchanged name of Jane Slade and Sons during the time of Samuel and John's joint ownership (Mr B Hall)

In 1911 Slades yard took on a commission from a Bristol pilot, George Morrice. In the dangerous waters of the Bristol Channel the pilots raced out to meet the incoming ships, the first one getting the job. A fast and well-built working craft was the lifeblood for a Bristol Pilot. The reputation of Slades yard must still have been high. The *Jane Slade* was well known, as were other Slade-built ships. The *Jane Slade* held the record for the fastest journey from St Michaels in the Azores to Bristol. After payment of £350 George Morrice took delivery of the boat and named her *Cornubia*, working her until she was sold as yacht in 1920. She is still in existence today, renamed Hirta, but in need of much care and attention as she sits in a yard at Gloucester Docks.

A smaller, but no doubt still welcome, commission in 1911 was the building of a new ferry for the route between Polruan and Fowey. There had been a petition signed by almost every resident of Polruan, complaining about the state of the ferry, as it was still just a small open rowing boat. The petition called for *boat powered by steam or other mechanical means*. Eventually it was agreed that a boat should be built and Slades yard was commissioned to build it. *The first motor ferry boat for Polruan was built by Ernest Slade to the Kelvin Company's own design. The engine was a seven-horse-power Kelvin and was installed by Donald Graham of Looe in* 1912.

So Ernie and his brothers were ship repairers, boat builders, blockmakers, and chandlers. The family tradition of responsibility within the local community continued, in 1910 the *Slade family of shipwrights* gave their orchard as a site and also a financial contribution towards the proposed Constitutional Hall. It was opened in 1912 and still remains in use as the village hall.

Thomas and Bodmin Asylum

Thomas was now back permanently in Bodmin in the private patients' building. Carew Building stands on its own in its own gardens within the Asylum complex. A few letters have survived from him to his daughter, Dora, aged 25 and earning her living. In this one written after the death of his brother, John (they were together in Bodmin) he refers to his children, Alfred, Frederick, Phillip and Ruby plus his old friend and brother in law, John Edward Hocken.

Cornwall County Asylum
Bodmin January 25th 1910
Tuesday afternoon
Dear Dora
I am writing in answer to your last letter to me after a long time. Should have written to you before if it had not been for your uncles death I am just as usual again and I must thank your good lady for sending me the six apples they were very nice and I enjoyed them.. Alfred, Phillip and Ruby was in to see me the Tuesday after Xmas and brought me a nice cake, oranges, apples and a piece of Pudding and your uncle John Edward sent me in 3 nice brighten cakes so I was well off for the time in eatables. It lasted me several day in the month. How did Fred spend his time with you all this Xmas, well I hope. I hope dear Dora you are going on allright in your new place and doing well. I hope you read your Bible and live a good life dont abuse your self in any way. I should like to hear you are a teacher in the Sunday school if your good people would allow you to do so. What do you get for a year if its a very good salary you might save something out of it for a rainy day as the saying is. Hoping your all well and in the best of good health. My best of love to you and believe me yours truly
      Father Thomas Slade

Excuse my writing, it is rather cold holding the pen in my fingers.

It may be that he was not alone, as the visitors' ledgers show Samuel in and out of the Asylum.

    31/1/10 Samuel Slade discharged on trial
    28/2/10 Samuel Slade discharged as recovered, private patient

    23/12/10 Samuel Slade a private patient. It is recommended that the rate of maintenance of the patient on re-admission be charged at 21/- as formerly

    29/5/11 Discharged on trial
    26/12/11 Discharged recovered

This might have been the energetic Samuel, but without access to the patient records it canot be verified.

1914 First World War

When the First World War broke out the Slade family were by now scattered. Christopher junior had retired to Fowey, Samuel was living in Fowey and Ernie was struggling to run the yard with his two brothers. Thomas was in Bodmin and his remaining sons and daughters were working. Dora had married a Royal Navy man, Robert Adams, the son of a local Fowey tobacconist in 1913 at Saltash. Even in his isolation in Bodmin, Thomas was well aware of events outside.

Carew Buildings
Bodmin
Dec 21st 14

My dear Dora,
*   I was pleased to get your unexpected letter, but was very pleased to have it on the 8th inst, and when I read its contents I was pleased that your dear Husband had been promoted chief petty officer and torpedo instructor and his brother Birtey too second lieutenant in the Royal Artillery. They are two good men, and smart with, and I do hope They will do well and when this Terrable so called war is over They will come home all safe and well. I was pleased to have your postcard saying that Ted had arrived at Bihea all safe and well. When Fred was hear in September he told me that your brother will be coming home to Polruan for this Xmas holiday if its convenient for Them to do so. My dear Dora can you manage to send me a few apples and oranges when you get this note from me. I should have written before now only I had this Paper given me today. I hope you will spend a happy Xmas together with my dear daughter in law Molly and dear little Gordon. My very best of love to you all, and again wishing you a very happy time together and a bright new year when it comes.*
*   And believe me yours Truly*
*   Father Thomas Slade*

Molly was the second wife of Dora's older brother, James Sidney Slade, now resident in Liverpool.

In February of 1915 his younger brother, Christopher junior, died. In his will he left £3068 4s 3d to his widow, Mary Ann (his second wife) and his daughter Annie. This was the largest sum left by any of the brothers. He had married twice and some of the money could have come from his first marriage, or it may have been an indication of good management. He owned several properties and does not seem to have risked any money on shares in ships. He obviously had made a good living from the inn and the coal business and he and his family had not had to pay for the cost of a stay in the asylum. These costs for the private patients could add up to a significant sum.

Holly House where Thomas retired - 'Ivy House' in The Loving Spirit (Christian du Maurier Browning)

Carew Buildings
Bodmin
Cornwall

Saturday evening 6pm
Mon 13.11.15

My dear Dora,

I received your postcard on the 1st inst for the same I was pleased to receive and note you said you were quite well which I was pleased to hear and I hope you are still keeping quite well. You must eat all the nourishing things you can get hold of so as you could gain more flesh on your body.

You say that Harry was there to see you the day before you sent me the postcard. I hope he is keeping well and please give him my best respects when you see him again and love as well, and he must keep up a good heart through all this dreadful war and we shall all come out all right in the end. When I heard from Ruby some 3 or 4 weeks ago they were all very well home that way I shall write Ruby again soon to know how they are getting on up to the present time. I see by the Papers that all the young men are to be called up so I expect Bill will have to be in it and if it was me I would rather volunteer than be made to join, it would be better for him to do it. Fred, I dont know what to say about him. If they want more men after all the young men are called up married men will have to go but he being in the Railway that is a Government job so he might be left where he is for the time being. Do you hear from any of them. When you get this write me as soon as you can. My best of love to you and Harry and hope you will always keep well while you are down that way.

I feel fairly well for the present. Yours truly and loving father
Thomas Slade
Dora could you send me some more envelopes like this your note is in.

Wartime Problems in the Yard

With the outbreak of war the yard, under Ernie's management, was having financial difficulties. Some of these problems seem to have started before the war. In May 1914 the County Asylum was chasing for payment of Thomas' private patients bills which were in arrears. These had reached £50 by October of that year. With Thomas' children now spread around the country, Ernie Slade was the guarantor for his bill payments. It is quite possible that he was in turn having difficulty getting payment from them. Getting payments from customers was also proving difficult; in 1914 Ernie claimed against the schooner *Thomas* for non-payment for repairs. Even the Hocken family, once major ship owners, owed money on the work for the ES *Hocken*. Although the cargoes had produced a profit of £820, the ship was already in debt for a large repair bill at Slades yard and so the family sold their interests to the then master Capt. Harry Martyn.

Throughout the war years, the asylum continued to chase Ernie for arrears:
1916 26/6 *No reply from the guarantor of* Mr. T. *Slade. Write again to* Mrs. E. C. *Slade of* East Street *and state that patient will be transferred to pauper wards unless due is paid.*
Two months later 1916 28/8 £22:6 *paid on account of* Mr. T. *Slade and recommended that unless balance of £27:6 is paid by end of quarter he be transferred.*
28/8 *Since meeting,* Balance received and patient move deferred.

Ernie was spending some money elsewhere; he began to buy up ships. These were often well known, but old, ships that were being sold cheaply. He was however, unlucky

The portrait of the Jane Slade painted at Livorno to celebrate her famous passage. The painting was given to Daphne du Maurier by the Slade family (private collection)

in his purchases, which must have continued the drain of the yard's finances. In 1916 he bought the *Ada Peard*, the master being his cousin, James Sidney Slade. His ownership was brief. She went ashore in the Salmon River, Nova Scotia in September 1918 and was condemned.

He was also having problems with other commitments. In December 1916 the clerk to the Harbour Commissioners wrote: *Dear Sir, I have to remind you that you have not attended a meeting of the Commissioners for 6 mths* and shortly after this they wrote again. His fellow commissioners, chaired by Sir Arthur Quiller Couch, decided to fill his position on the Board but in their letter, they referred directly to his business. *Seat now vacant but taking into consideration the difficulties which the Commissioners know you have experienced in your business owing to the war.* They did however elect him to the casual vacancy. His attendance remained a problem through the war and in the end in 1918 they lost patience. 1918 14th Jan from the Harbour Commissioners to EC Slade. He was *asked to attend meeting or seat is vacant again.* 1918 23rd August Letter to EC Slade: *Unanimous election in place of Ernest Slade of Sam Slade to Harbour Commissioners.*

However, despite his business difficulties, Slades yard still had an excellent reputation:

I then made up my mind to go in for a ship of my own. I came to Fowey with the 'Utopia', Mr. Slade, my friend, advised me to buy the brigantine 'Raymond' from the joiners at Whitstable, Mr. Slade said he would rig her out for me as a barquentine and right well he did his work and made a splendid job of it. He made all her yards and rigging new, had all the sails repaired and did everything that was required, put a new motor winch on her deck.

This ship was originally built in 1876 in Prince Edward Island. On completion of the work, she was re-registered in Fowey on 20th January 1916. She later became the *Lady Quirk*.

Carew Buildings - Bodmin Asylum - occupied by Thomas Slade and others as private patients (Author)

Death of Thomas

On Christmas Day 1917 Thomas Slade died. He was 80 years old. The parish records show that he was buried at Lanteglos parish church, but there is no sign of any headstone for him. Probate was granted in April 1918 to his remaining executor, his brother, *Samuel Slade shipwright*. Thomas' will ensured that all properties, shares etc. could be realised and the resulting monies divided among his children. His effects were valued at £934 13s 4d. Samuel, as executor, sold Thomas' house on Fore Street Polruan, Holly House, for £260 to James Sidney Slade. James may have been attempting to provide for his younger sister. Dora had just had her first child, a daughter, Gladys and moved to Holly House. Samuel acquired the 19 shares in the Jane Slade.

A brief family reunion was occasioned by the combination of the war and Thomas' death. His third son by his first marriage, Samuel, had moved some years before to Australia, moving from jobs in mining to the railways. Now in the army he was able to delay his departure due to his father's death. After the war Samuel returned to Australia, sadly committing suicide in 1930 age 60. As Thomas died his ship was still sailing out of Fowey. The *Jane Slade* had sailed right through the First World War frequently sailing to the Normandy coast; her master throughout was H Smith of Polruan. With the ending of the Great War, many of the Polruan residents and the men returning from war must have hoped for better times to come. Ernie as the manager of the yard and his brothers, Jim and Joe looked ahead to new opportunities.

The Jane Slade
painted by
Chappell after
1905, after the
third mast
was added
(Mrs J Adams)

8
An End and a Beginning

It was custom in Plyn and generally in the west country, to have terms of long credit. Folk trusted one another, and did not bother to send their account at quarterly dates, but waited until they had a need for their money, knowing that the necessary sum would be immediately forthcoming. The Coombes for generations had followed this old-standing custom, and had never found it at fault. They had always known with whom they were dealing, and orders went by word of mouth, and never by written contract

Optimistic forecasts suggested that better times were coming, trade would pick up and cargoes would need to be moved. Ernie continued to buy sailing ships, but not just any ship, he looked for those that had a good reputation for speed. On 22nd June 1918 he registered the *Trevellas*, a 127-ton schooner. Built in Hayle in 1876, her speed was well known in the merchant community. One month later he sold the majority of the shares in her to the Kearon family of Arklow, but retained eight shares in her. He remained as her managing owner until 1925.

Management, however, did not seem to be Ernie's strong point. He was still the recipient of letters from the Harbour Commissioners. This time the complaints were about the constant overloading of the Polruan ferry, now owned by Slade and Sons. Then there were the logs that had been left on Mixtow Beach which had not been removed, despite previous requests. These logs were the remains of the old Bodinnick horse ferry, now replaced by a newly-built motorised version built by Slade and Sons.

The 127-ton schooner Trevellas, *built in 1876, bought by Ernest Slade in 1918 (S Kearon)*

Harry Adams, husband of Dora Slade, friend of Daphne du Maurier, and the author's grandfather

At least the war was over, now surely life could return to what it had been? But the old life of the port had changed, for many the reality of post war life in Cornwall was unemployment. Cornwall was suffering from a severe crisis in mining. The population was declining as families left for better opportunities. Even the dependable china clay industry, upon which the harbour of Fowey was reliant, was suffering. In 1921 and 1922, as Phillip Payton points out, there was *fearful hardship in the villages of the clay country*. In Polruan work was hard to find.

Harry Adams was one of the local men who returned from war. Harry was married to Thomas Slade's daughter, Dora. Their first child, Gladys, had been born in 1917 six months before Thomas died. Harry had been born in Leith, Scotland, but his parents had moved to Fowey and set up a tobacconist's shop in Fore Street. At the age of fourteen he had joined the Royal Navy, serving with distinction during the Battle of Jutland. Now retiring on a limited pension, he must have hoped, like all the other men, that work would return to the port. This was a view shared by the shipbrokers of the port. They were also looking at the possibility of improved freight rates as the trade routes reopened.

The AB Sherman

Freight rates did indeed rise steeply at the end of the war and firms scrambled to get hold of any vessel that was capable of carrying freight. Toyne Carter, a Fowey-based shipbroker, were among the many who sought ways to capitalise on the boom. In Plymouth in September 1919, they purchased a war prize: the three-masted American ship AB *Sherman* in Plymouth. She had been caught just off the Scillies handing fuel to the Germans.

Toyne Carter decided to bring her to Fowey and get J Slade and Sons to handle the repair work. This caused great excitement and comment in the village of Polruan. A large work force would be needed for this very significant commission. The AB *Sherman* would be the largest ship ever to be repaired in the Port of Fowey. The men of Slades yard had an excellent reputation for their work. Ernie and his brothers saw this as the chance to put J Slade & Sons onto a firm footing, with the money they could build a permanent dry dock for repair work. At 622-tons and 177 feet long the ship was too large for the existing yard, so the decision was made to utilise Pont Pill as a dock area. She was brought from Plymouth and beached the other side of Brazen Island. Ernie was resourceful and got hold of an ex-army hut and set it up just above the beach as a workshop. Extra men were taken onto the payroll and work commenced. The work was going to take some time; Toyne Carter wanted a Lloyds A1 classification. The war damage had to be repaired, and this was significant as one man later recalled, she had been holed on both sides and her foremast had been damaged. In addition, originally three-masted she would be altered to four. While the yard was at full stretch they still managed to continue other work. In 1920 they made repairs to the schooner *Uncle Ned*. Built in 1867 in Ipswich, she was owned by R Kearon of Arklow and the master was W Kearon. The Kearons were a large family of mariners and shipowners and were to be associated with the Slade business in other ways. They had purchased the majority interest in *Trevellas* and at this time George Kearon became master of the *Jane Slade* remaining with her for the next three years. So Slades yard worked on with a small army of carpenters and shipwrights on the AB *Sherman* and other work.

The AB Sherman *on her sea trials in 1920/21 after being repaired in Slades yard (Fred Kitto)*

Post-war Changes

Jane and Christopher's last surviving child, Samuel, watched over these happenings from Fowey. He was aged 73 and living at 57 Esplanade directly opposite the old yard beside the quay. One last change came in September 1919 when he signed a 21-year lease of the Russell Inn, to the St Austell brewers, Walter Hicks. The incumbent landlord was Samuel's nephew, John Bate Slade, who had taken over the pub from his father, Christopher junior. With the change of management, John went back to sea after an unsuccessful attempt to persuade the Harbour Commissioners to appoint him as harbourmaster.

Ten months later on 6th July 1920, Samuel died - the last of Jane and Christopher's children. In his will he gave his occupation as shipbuilder, one of many occupations he could have chosen, but this was the one that meant most to him. His funeral was reported in the *Royal Cornwall Gazette*:

A *native of Polruan, one of a firm of Messrs. Slade and Sons, ship builders. He was the only surviving son, Captain T. Slade, Messrs. William, Christopher, John & Phillip having predeceased him. He was clerk to the schoolboard all through its existence. Funeral was attended by Ernest, James & Joseph Slade (nephews) Reg. Roberts and T. Slade (great nephews) Mrs. T. J. Roberts, Mrs. J. Roberts, Miss Norah Slade, Mrs. Sidney Samuel (nieces).*

The New Man of Business

Ernie was now the senior member of the Slade shipbuilding and repair business. All through this time the work on the AB *Sherman* continued. At last after some 20 months the work was completed in autumn of 1921 and now 4-masted, she was registered at Fowey. She was thoroughly surveyed by Lloyds and an A1 certificate for six years was achieved. The cost of the work was £6535. By now cargoes were few, during the time the men of Slades yard had toiled on her the market conditions had changed *what had been an acute shortage of ships when she had been bought was fast becoming a surplus.* Ward Jackson in his research for his book on the ships of Fowey discovered that *she had cost £16,627 and £6536 had been spent on her, yet in November 1921 she was valued independently at £1,100. Worse was to come. In the spring of November 1922, arriving at Leghorn with china clay, water was found to have got into her cargo. In serious difficulties, she had to be sold to Italians. She realised £500! In England, her register was closed in November 1923. She had traded on Toyne Carter's account for only a few months. Refitted she had cost them £23,162, while her losses on voyage account were £25,000. She had put her owners out of pocket by some £48,000!*

The tragedy of the AB *Sherman* very nearly sank the firm of Toyne Carter. They managed to survive by becoming a limited liability company and lasted in this state until they eventually were acquired by English China Clays in 1977. A small family business like Slades had no chance. Small firms like theirs worked on long lines of credit. As Toyne Carter was unable or refused to pay, their creditors began to put pressure on them. The recession of the 1920s was beginning to bite and other firms were also in trouble with Fowey Coaling & Ship Repair Company going into liquidation in 1924.

After 1922 Slades did little work. The bank put in a receiver who remained till the war and then the yard was idle throughout. Freddie Ricketts born in 1902 recalled that he was apprenticed to Slades in 1916 for seven years. By 1922, there was no work in yard when it found that Toyne Carter could not meet the bill. The men of Slades had their pay cut to 50/- a week. Many of them began looking for other work. Matters were desperate. The men taken on in such high hopes were laid off. Feelings in Polruan were strong, to this day the loss of the AB *Sherman* is a sensitive topic. Work at the yard was welcome from anywhere and of any size. The only other yard in the harbour was Hellers yard in Caffa Mill Pill at Fowey, Butsons having closed down in 1910. In1922 Slades yard built the *Maya* for the shipbrokers Hannan Samuel. Jack Samuel recalled: *My father had a new motor boat built by J Slade & Sons in 1922 – an 18 footer called 'Maya' - which cost £90. It was not much used as father was not mechanical. Eventually she was only kept for 3 years and then sold to Freddy Johns for £100 who used her as his pilot boat for the next 30 odd years.*

Ernie and his brothers worked to put the firm back on its feet and pay off their creditors. In 1920 Tregaskes had sold Newquay Dock to a steamship company from Bristol, Alfred J Smith Ltd. This was potentially a big problem for when Slades' lease ran out they might not be able to gain access to a wet dock, an essential facility for many repairs. They still owned the yard below East Street, close to the main town quay. Here craft could be pulled up out of the water to be worked on. In June 1923, Ernie continued his purchase of older vessels. He bought and registered the 177-ton *Thames*. She was described on her initial registration in Fowey as an *Auxiliary Motor Screw Vessel*. Two months later she was re-registered after completion of the work to alter her to a *square stern brigantine(sailing)*. He sold shares to Charles Rundle, master mariner, George Kearon, Polruan mariner, Thomas Dunstan, Fowey hotel proprietor and to Sydney Samuel, Fowey shipbroker. The last named being the same man for whom they had built the *Maya*. This brought Ernie's ship management total up to three, including the *Jane Slade* and the *Trevellas*.

Despite Ernie's efforts, Slades yard was now so deep in trouble that by 1924 they needed outside help. John Keay was a chartered accountant working in St Austell. He had arrived in 1922 from Stoke on Trent to take charge of the branch office for Bourner Bullock. The main reason he had been brought to St Austell by his employers was due to the large amount of work from the varied china clay companies. These small firms were too small to make profits in the changed economy and were rapidly amalgamating into the new English China Clays. This work for a number of clay producers and merchants gave him an insight into the general problems of the china clay industry. He was to join the board of ECC in 1929 becoming one of its most famous and formative managing directors. Meanwhile in 1924 he was appointed to draw up a deed of arrangement between J Slade and Sons and their creditors:

An Indenture of Conveyance & assignment dated 15 April 1924 (registered under deeds of arrangement act 1914) made between EC Slade, JC Slade & JE Slade trading in co partnership under the style or firm of J Slade & Sons

It then mentions some of the names of the creditors, William James Adams, H Hannah and John Blain and *the several persons companies & partnership firms whose names were scheduled being creditors.*

The Deed of Arrangement was potentially the best option for all. With John Keay's help, they had persuaded their creditors that the best chance of receiving any money was to leave them in business rather than force a bankruptcy. The Deed of Arrangement listed the funds, some tied up in property both business and personal, that was security against the debts. Ernie together with his brothers, Joe and Jim, had joint assets worth £4478 9s 8d. Jim had no additional assets, but Ernie had £350 (including £135 in property) and Joe had £200 of which £140 was in property. Samuel, who was included as a partner up to his death in 1922, had £1000 of property set against the debts. The amount of the debt was £4198 7s 9d, a significant sum and only just covered by the business value. It left no funds for any type of investment in the yard. It may have been some small consolation that they had managed to avoid the spectre of bankruptcy, but there was very little left and the heart had gone out of the business. Property not immediately related to the business had to be sold.

While Samuel had died in 1922, his widow found that his estate was still liable. On 18th November 1925, the Russell Inn was sold to Walter Hicks & Co (St Austell Ales) for £500. Just five years before its value, as estimated by the Inland Revenue, had been £780. It had been in Slade hands for nearly 90 years. As a footnote it is worth noting that the sale also required the signature of the wife of Sir Arthur Quiller Couch. Dame Louisa had inherited a small mortgage of £189 on the Russell Inn from her mother and this had been cleared by Samuel in 1894. This mortgage was what remained of the £200 taken out by William Salt in 1847 to help finance Christopher Slade's first shipyard.

Another asset on the books, was the *Jane Slade*. George Kearon had been her master since 1919, sailing her out of Fowey around the coast. Unlike her earlier days when the crew were almost all local men, the crew now were from Dublin, Colchester, Newport, Peterborough and Penzance. In August 1923 George Kearon was replaced by WH Cort and a new crew was taken on. Among the crew were three young men on their first ship, R Martyn, Fred Rickett and Sid Lee. Fred had been a carpenter with Slades yard and possibly the two others as well. The end of work at the yard encouraged them to try a new career at sea, it did not last long. WH Cort was to be the last master of the *Jane Slade*. He was an uncertificated master, which was still permissible in the coastal trade. Later he became well known as the last master of a west country sailing ship, the *Waterwitch*. The *Jane Slade* spent her last few years around the British coast; London, Hull, Plymouth, Fowey and on occasions crossing the channel to Antwerp. Keast in his *History of Fowey* says that *finally when bound from Hull to a west country port, she went aground and was later brought home for repairs, but after being laid up in Pont Pill, she was gradually dismantled.* There is no evidence of an instance of her going aground in the available log books which show her last passages as from London on 7th July 1924, arriving in Fowey on 6th November 1924 via Cardiff, Kirkaldy, Queensferry and Hull.

For nearly 55 years she had been a regular sight in the harbour, now she was laid up, still fully rigged, in Pont Pill near where the men had worked so hard and with such enthusiasm on the ill-fated AB *Sherman*. Perhaps Ernie hoped he might still one day get some work for her, but she remained in Pont untouched as a legacy of their past.

The Writers

Among the visitors coming in ever greater numbers to visit the picturesque port of Fowey was Gerald du Maurier. He and his family were looking for a second home. They found one in Bodinnick in 1926. They bought Swiss Cottage, previously a ship building yard where John Marks, George Nickels and the Butsons had worked. The du Mauriers renamed the house Ferryside. Daphne, in particular, was strongly attracted to the local area. She explored all along the harbour and across the cliffs. On one of her walks along the side of Pont Pill, she discovered the *Jane Slade* still mostly intact and with her figurehead of a woman. Her imagination was captured by the ship, its location and the men and especially the woman who had created her. Daphne needed information and asked her new-found friend, Harry Adams. Harry had been employed as a boatman to her father and taught Daphne to row, to fish, to sail. He took her hunting for conger eels and shooting rabbits - a way of life dramatically different from her lifestyle in London.

She was asking the right man. Harry, as the son-in-law of Thomas Slade, was able to give her the full story. His wife, Dora, granddaughter of Jane had been born just a few months before Jane had died, but the ship had always been a part of her life. She had watched as a young child from her home on the Esplanade as her father came home on board the *Jane Slade*. Dora recalled how she would slip out from the house to the end of the garden and sit on the steps by the harbour, dipping her feet into the water. These memories were valuable, but Daphne wanted more information. Where had the ship sailed to, what had she carried, was there anyone who could recall Jane herself? Harry introduced Daphne to Ernie Slade who was still the owner of the ship. Ernie had been only 17 when his grandmother, Jane had died and may have had some memory of her. If not Ernie, then certainly there would have been many other people in the village with firsthand knowledge of Jane - the Jane who becomes Janet Coombe in *The Loving Spirit*, who had the first say and the last say at the yard, who longed to be boy and go to sea. Jane who had a ship built for her and named after her.

Slades yard at this time still did the occasional small piece of work, building the 10-ton motor cutter *Majub* for Captain Collins, the harbourmaster in 1928. Daphne, by now, captivated by the legend of Jane and her ship also craved a boat for herself - to be built by Jane's descendants in the same yard. She did not find this an easy task, Jane's descendants were not to be hurried. At last, Daphne witnessed the launching of her own ship when the 7-ton yacht the *Marie Louise* was launched.

Meanwhile, her heroine's ship was reaching her fate. In the same year Daphne took delivery of her yacht, the Business Development Company, based at Cross Lane, St Austell, had taken over all of the remaining shares in the *Jane Slade*. Probably part of the final arrangements for finalising the business affairs, the shares cannot have been worth much if anything. In December 1928 the *Jane Slade* entry on the Fowey Ships Register was closed. The final register of shares was:

William Geake	7	RJ Sobey	1	JE Hocken	1	TH Slade	3
W & T Pearce	4	Eliza Carell	2	EC Slade	4	A & E Cordell	2
Ethel Daniel	6	Business Dev Co Ltd	33				

The *Jane Slade* was gradually dismantled. Her rigging was removed, all items were cleared out from her and finally her figurehead was removed. The bare bones were left to rot on the mud of Pont Pill. Harry Adams arranged with Ernie that Daphne, who had such a strong feeling for the ship, be given the figurehead and it was positioned at Ferryside below her bedroom.

If the yard was in its death throes and the ship itself was dismantled, Daphne would ensure that the legend remained. In the winter of 1929, Daphne stayed in Bodinnick to write her first book, working in her room above the figurehead of her inspiration. Ernie and Harry provided letters, papers, business documents. Friends and neighbours found books to provide background information. She wrote on, the first part came easily as she charted Janet and Joseph Coombe's lives. These were the two based on Jane Slade and her son, Thomas, about whom she had most information to play with. She found the last part the hardest, but here she was not only bringing it into the present, having to rely very heavily on her imagination for the characters, but she was writing about events to which she was a personal witness. At last on Tuesday, March 30th the book was finished. It came to a staggering 200,000 words.

Slades yard by now was idle, although they were still advertising as boatbuilders and chandlers in 1930. Daphne described what she saw:

Low tide at Pont, showing all that remains of the many ships left there (Christian du Maurier Browning)

The shipbuilding yard of Thomas Coombe and Sons was empty of timber and gear. There was no longer the clanging of the hammer, nor the high pitched song of the saw. Ships must go elsewhere to be re-classed, yachtsmen must wander farther up the harbour in search of a designer for their craft. The shed in the corner of the yard was taken over by an engineer in need of premises;... The loft building had not been sold, the big wide loft where Thomas Coombe and his sons had chipped and chiselled at their models. His namesake and grandson Thomas, together with his Cousin James, still clung to this place as a last remnant of their departed trade, but they used it no longer as a workshop and as a dwelling of inspiration, but as a boat store, humble and insignificant.

In 1931 on February 23rd T*he Loving Spirit* was published. It received favourable reviews and was also published in America. Daphne had achieved her ambition, a published author and the beginnings of an independent income. Her book reached a wide audience with it stirring tales of life at sea. Tommy Browning, a serving army officer, enjoyed it so much he visited Fowey and asked to be introduced to the author. Daphne's link with Jane was to become even stronger when one year later she married Tommy Browning in Lanteglos Church, one hundred and one years after the marriage of Christopher and Jane.

While Daphne left Bodinnick to start her new life as an army wife, the depression of the 1930s was continuing to bite. Another writer arrived in Polruan. Leo Walmsley described his impression of Polruan in 1933:

This had been the time of the post-Kaiser depression, when more than three quarters of Britain's merchant fleet was laid up, when Cornwall's china clay industry was at a standstill, and practically the whole male population of Polruan was unemployed and on the dole.

Walmsley had come to the area to escape creditors. Ernie Slade let him rent the old army hut in Pont Pill, last used by the Slades when they had been repairing the A B S*herman*. He, like Daphne, was inspired by the area. His life in the old Army hut beside the Fowey river was written into his book L*ove in the Sun*, a thinly disguised story of his time in Polruan and the people he met, including the Slades. It was published to critical acclaim at the outbreak of war. Leo Walmsley left the area shortly afterwards, but returned to the same spot after the war and in his second book based in Polruan P*aradise Creek*, this time non-fiction, he relates the last days of the yard:

The Slades were already bankrupt, carrying on in possession of their idle yard only by the grace of their creditors. Charley Toms himself was on the dole. Then slowly the depression began to lift, rising eventually to the boom, which preceded the beginnings of the Second World War. The boom came too late to save the firm of Slades. The three brothers who owned it, Charley, Jimmy and Ernie were old men. Part of the yard was taken over by a firm of boatbuilders who had a yard up the river. The rest, a disused dock and a stone building adjoining the blacksmiths forge was leased to my old friend Charley Toms. With the financial backing of friends a private company was formed. The dock was filled in and a slip made for the hauling up of fair-sized craft for repair. In addition a new shed had been built, equipped

with power saws and planing machines. Charley Toms was now the port's principal yacht and small boat builder, employing more than 30 men including many of those who had worked for Slades.

When Ernie, Jim and Joe Slade had retired, beaten by the economics of the situation, there was a final attempt by the fourth generation to continue the family business. Sam Slade, Joe's son, still lives in Polruan, the last Slade in the village. He recalls how Jim's son, Tom Slade, tried for while to keep going, but he eventually gave up and left to live in Ireland selling the yard for £600. He seems to have sold to his cousin, as the deeds show the yard being sold by TJ Slade in 1938 to Mr JWL Thomas. This looks like the adopted son of Ernie. Ernie's eldest sister Jane Thomas had died leaving him to bring up her daughter, Phyllis and son, John. Finally, just a few years later, in April 1943, the yard and the house below East Street were sold to Mrs D Browning. It was in her name and not jointly with her husband. Daphne du Maurier now owned Jane Slade's yard, yet another link with Jane. She went into partnership with Norman Hunkin who ran the yard until 1967. Why did she buy the yard? Perhaps to provide work for Polruan or to maintain a link with Jane. Whatever the reason, a significant benefit was to an old friend, Ernie Slade. It enabled him, now in poor health, to remain in his home in East Street above his old yard. Today this yard is now Toms yard, started by Charlie Toms the grandfather of the current owners who was originally the blacksmith for the Slades.

Toms have expanded along to Brazen Island, recreating and extending the line of yards that were once all run by the Slades.

In 1943 Daphne wrote a letter of condolence to Mrs Dora Adams; Harry Adams had died. She had been planning to write to him *and tell him about my new book, which he would have enjoyed, a story of adventure in Cornwall, but now, alas, it is too late. I shall never forget the good days we had together, and how he would take me fishing and rabbiting, and he taught me to row and to sail too. If I shut my eyes it seems like yesterday and off we would go in the rowing boat Annabelle Lee and look for pollack outside the harbour. And if it had not been for him I could never have written my first book 'The Loving Spirit', because he showed me all those old letters of the Slade family. I will always remember him with real affection.* In Harry she had found a good companion, a well-read man with a strong sense of humour. He was generous with his time and whatever else he had. His wife, Dora, remembered how he had caught a large conger eel. By the time he reached home there was hardly any of it left as he cut pieces off for friends and neighbours on the way. Harry and Dora had lived with their three children in a variety of rented properties in Polruan. On one occasion when comment had been made about the large number of house moves, his reply was that *some folk do a tour of the world, we are doing a tour of Polruan*!

At the end of the Second World War when Leo Walmsley returned to live in Pont Pill, he went to see Ernie, who was bedridden living in the old Slade house above Hunkins yard:

Pont Beach as described by Leo Walmsley in Love in the Sun *(Christian du Maurier Browning)*

in the rowing boat Annabel Lee & look for pollack outside the harbour. And if it had not been for him I could never have written my first book "The Loving Spirit", because he showed me all those old letters of the Slade family. I shall always remember him with real affection.

I remained watching him for a while. It was a comfortable room, rugs on the floor, a fire in the grate, more pictures of sailing ships on the walls a vase of anemones on the bedside table, everything spotlessly clean. But it was not luxurious, as it would have been if he had been rich. Dear Ernie. He had failed only because he lacked what it takes to be a successful businessman. Like his two brothers he was a master craftsman, a shipwright and builder of boats. He had taken a delight and a pride in his craftsmanship, and he was never to be hurried, even to please a wealthy and sometimes exasperated customer. A job had to be done right to satisfy himself. He was devoid of greed. He expected a fair reward for his skill and labour-no more. And above all he was kind, tender generous, without spite or jealousy, fair minded, scrupulously honest and good humoured.

On 19th September 1949 Ernie died. He had struggled against many odds to maintain the legacy of Christopher, Jane and Samuel. He left little, just £142 15s 8d, *to his dear wife, Emma Louise Slade*. His simple one line will was witnessed by Norman Hunkin and his wife. His chosen executor was David Adams, the son of Harry and Dora.

David was back in his home village after wartime service in the Royal Navy. David served with another writer, a poet, who was to become very well known. Charles Causley and David became friends, and he in his turn came to Polruan and wrote a short story. Published in 1951 the story tells of a wartime friendship between two men who meet in the Royal Navy. One man suffers badly from seasickness and is taken under the wing of Walter 'Fanny' Adams. Adams looks forward to his return to his wife and child, his Cornish village and the boatyard that belongs to his family. War separates them, but the power of the memory causes the friend to travel to Cornwall to search for the village and his friend. The title is *Looking for Fanny*, published in his book of short stories *Hands To Dance*.

Gladys, David and Patricia; the three children of Harry and Dora, whom Daphne knew as young children living at Holly House, Polruan

This small family business based in a Cornish village has left a strong legacy. Many of their ships still exist in ship portraits; the legend of Jane, Christopher and Thomas and their ship remains in the fiction that started the career of a well-known writer, and the last days of the yard provided shelter and background material for another author. Even after Slades yard was finished it provided one more inspiration for a writer later to become a renowned poet. From an historical perspective the Slade business, comprising as it did: ship-building, repair, maintenance, owning and management; coal trading, innkeeping and master mariners, was unique in the area. When Christopher started his business, there were at least three other local ship-builders: Nickels, Brokenshaw and Butson. The business outlasted all of them and was wider in scope. The Slades' 'flagship' the *Jane Slade* had a strong reputation as one of the fastest ships of her time, They built the largest ships if not the greatest number. Slades and their men were a part of a long tradition of skilled craftsmen who provided wooden vessels to meet local demand until, like so many other yards, the inter-war slump and the new world of steam and steel overwhelmed them.

It is Jane, herself, however who stands out as the central figure - the woman who dominates the story in fact as in fiction. Christopher began the yard, but Jane was there beside him. On his death she came to the fore, managing all the strands of the various businesses and remaining in control until her death. Thomas, Samuel and Ernie each in their own way endeavoured to maintain Jane's legacy and passed the story on with the help of Harry Adams. All of these people are gone and their ships no longer at sea, but something still remains. Jane is a part of the harbour today, watching from her vantage point beside the Bodinnick Ferry, as she has done for so many years. Her spirit continues to inspire.

Appendices

1
Du Maurier connections - the story of T*he Loving Spirit*

Du Maurier's book T*he Loving Spirit* tells the story of three generations of the Coombe family, who live in Plyn, Cornwall. Plyn is largely based on Polruan with a little of Fowey added.

It begins with Janet Coombe who marries her cousin Thomas at Lanoc church in 1830. This is Lanteglos parish church where Daphne, herself, was to be married. Their two eldest sons follow Thomas into his shipbuilding business, but Joseph goes to sea and later qualifies as a master mariner. He and his mother, Janet, share a close bond with one another and their love of the sea. The Inn is never mentioned, but Janet's strong influence and control of the yard is highlighted.

Thomas and his sons build their most important ship the *Janet Coombe* which has a figurehead modelled on Janet. Joseph is to be her first master. Janet dies early in a dramatic moment as the ship is launched. She still, however, remains a powerful presence for the rest of the book as it seems her spirit goes into the ship. The story then follows Joseph and his strained relationship with his eldest son, Christopher, who he hopes will follow him as master of the *Janet Coombe*. But Christopher hates the sea.

Christopher gets work in London and marries there. His father meanwhile suffers a breakdown and goes to Sudmin Asylum. When later, Christopher returns to Cornwall he is too late to see his father who, on release from Sudmin, has drowned. He finds that his uncle, Philip, has become increasingly powerful and Philip is to play a fateful part in the downfall of the family shipyard. Christopher returns to work in the shipyard with his cousins and his third child, Jennifer, is born in Plyn. When Christopher dies helping to save the *Janet Coombe* and her crew from shipwreck, Jennifer and her mother return to London.

It is Jennifer who later returns to Plyn and just as Daphne did, she explores the wreck of the *Janet Coombe* and the graves in Lanoc church. The story ends with the death of Great Uncle Philip and the marriage of Jennifer to her cousin, John. They live over the shipyard with the figurehead of Janet Coombe watching over them.

When I was a young girl, I wrote to Daphne du Maurier to ask her about the history of my family. I quote her reply in full:

> April 1st. 1967.
> *Menabilly*
> *Par*
> *Cornwall*

Dear Miss Doe,
Thank you for your letter. I am so interested to hear you want to find out about your family tree, and I only wish I had kept the old papers and letters out of which I composed The Loving Spirit. You will realise the novel was written

Daphne du
Maurier's letter to
the author, which
started the search
for information on
the Slades

MENABILLY
PAR
CORNWALL

Dear Miss Doe,

Thank you for your letter.

I am so interested to hear you want to find

out about your family tree, and I only wish I had

.... of which

Yours sincerely,

[signature: Daphne du Maurier Browning]

nearly 40 years ago, and my memory is hazy about genuine details. You ought to be able to find the graves of various members of the Slade family in Lanteglos churchyard.

The geneological table in the book is correct in parts. The family starts with Thomas who married Janet - (Thomas and Janet Coombe) The real names were Christopher Slade who married Jane Slade, who gave her name to the schooner, and whose figurehead hangs above my sister's house Ferryside, Bodinnick. They had a large family, and the Joseph Coombe in the book corresponds to Thomas Slade, Janet's son, who becomes the skipper of the Jane Slade. I think I am right in thinking Captain Tom _did_ marry twice, like the Captain Joseph in the book, but I could be wrong in this.

I am pretty sure he had a son Herbert (not Christopher) and others, also a daughter who corresponds with the daughter Katherine (daughter of Captain Joseph) in the book. This Katherine would be your grandmother, who married Mr Adams your dear grandfather, who taught me to row and to fish, and was our boatman for so many years. I cannot now remember where Ernie and Jim Slade come in the family tree, and to whom they correspond in the book, but they were the last of the Slades to run the Slade boatyard at Polruan, with their nephew (?) cousin (?) John Thomas, who was the great grandson of Jane and Christopher Slade, and from whom I bought the Yard towards the middle or the end of the last war. I am not sure whether he is still alive. The actual story is, of course, fictitious, except for the fact that the schooner was built at the yard, named after Jane, and skippered by the son Captain Tom, who was a great character. (Your great grandfather.) There was no wicked son Philip. He was a figment of my imagination! The character of Jennifer was also imaginary, and introduced by me to bring the story up to date in modern times and to marry her second cousin John, thus completing the family tree. I am quite sure there are no skeletons in the cupboard! Ivy House was the old family home. I am not sure of the correct name, but it stands on the left-hand side (sic) of Polruan hill (looking up the hill from the harbour) a little way back from the street.

At the end of the book I make Jennifer and John live in the house that is part of the boat-yard, but here I was imagining my sister's house Ferryside.

It is very sad that the Slades Yard, later Hunkin's Yard, has had to be sold for financial reasons, and I only hope the new owners will continue to run it as a boatyard.

Do remember me to your mother Gladys.
Yours sincerely,
Daphne du Maurier Browning

Daphne du Maurier signing copies of her book in the branch of Boots lending library above the Boots chemist shop in Fowey (Graham Gullick)

Characters

Thomas Coombe
Thomas is based on Christopher Slade, founder of the yards. While Thomas remains as a broken man after the death of his wife, Janet, Christopher died just months before his great ship was due to be launched.

Janet Coombe
Janet (1811-1863) is based on Jane Slade (1813-1885). In the book there is no mention of the Russell Inn. Daphne may not have been aware of her connection with it, although it had only recently left Slade ownership. What Daphne did understand was Jane's powerful influence through the years (in the 1920s there would have been plenty of people, including Ernie Slade who could recall Jane, 35 to 40 years later). One of the most dramatic moments of the book is Janet's death, the event that enables her to continue as the spirit of the ship to influence later generations.

Samuel Coombe
Samuel follows his father, Thomas, into the yard, as indeed did his real life counterpart. William Salt Slade, eldest-surviving son of Jane followed Christopher into the yard and spent his whole life building and maintaining ships. William married Susan Rowe and they had a large family.

Herbert Coombe
Herbert and his brother, Samuel run the yard after their father's death. Herbert marries Elsie Hoskett and has a very large family. This is based on John Slade who married Ann Hanson, but the large family was that of his older brother, William (Samuel Coombe), who had 12 children.

Philip Coombe
Youngest son of Janet and Thomas, he is 'quite the gentleman' and the man of business. While Daphne was at pains

to explain that Philip was a figment of her imagination, his career, if not his character, owes a significant amount to that of Samuel Slade. Samuel was known as 'quite the gentleman'.

Elizabeth Coombe
Younger daughter of Janet and Thomas, she marries Nicholas Stevens, a local farmer. She is possibly based on Elizabeth who married John Edward Hocken, the sailmaker.

Joseph Coombe
Joseph is the favoured son of Janet, marries Susan Collins and on her death, Annie Tabb. Modelled on Thomas Slade. The comparison is very faithful, Thomas was said to be his mother's favourite. He also married twice, first Mary Tadd and then Ann Bate. He was admitted to the Bodmin Asylum. His career as Harbourmaster, however, was omitted.

Christopher Coombe
Christopher, son of Joseph, hates the sea and deserts the ship. He marries a Londoner, Bertha Parkins and has two sons and a daughter. There are no direct comparisons, except that George, son of Thomas and Ann, did move to London after a time at sea. He married a Londoner, Gladys, and they had one child, Dora. They settled in Streatham where they ran a tobacconist's shop.

Katherine Coombe
Said by Daphne to be based on Dora, daughter of Thomas and wife of Harry Adams. The relationship between Katherine and her young stepmother, Annie, has echoes in the relationship between Dora and Rebecca Collings. When Dora's mother died, it was Rebecca, the young housekeeper, who looked after her and her siblings. Rebecca later married Dora's older half brother, Thomas Herbert Slade, a marriage that did not please Dora.

Tom and James Coombe
Grandsons of Janet and Thomas Coombe, who were 'men over 50 who had been boys during the great shipbuilding boom'. Based on Ernie, Jim and Joe who were the sons of John Slade and grandsons of Jane and Christopher. These three would have been able to tell Daphne of the days of the great shipbuilding, two of them feature in the photograph of the yard and its men.

Janet Coombe
The ship and her career as fictionalised, are generally true to the real *Jane Slade*. She is mentioned in the fruit trade to the Azores and that she is known to be fast sailing vessel, for 'Joseph was desperate carrier of sail, pressing his little vessel under every rag he could set'. Reference is then made to the end of the fruit trade and the *Janet Coombe* goes to Newfoundland and the salt cod market. This was probably a misconception that was passed onto Daphne, as the *Jane Slade* never went into this latter trade. The letter quoted in the book from Samuel Coombe to his brother, has a familiar ring to it, and may well have been based on correspondence still available at the time.

Locations

Plyn, is Polruan with a bit of Fowey. Philip Coombe's house and office is based on Thomas and Ann's home at 43 Esplanade, Fowey. Ivy House, home of the Coombes is Holly House in Fore Street, Polruan. It is here that Thomas retired and it was later lived in by Harry Adams and his family. Daphne stayed there briefly. The main yard is still in Polruan beside the Quay, now owned by Toms and sons, although the ending of the book is based on Daphne's home, Ferryside. Lanoc church is Lanteglos church, St Wyllow. The castle, which features in the book, is probably Polruan Castle placed in the position of St Saviours, on the headland.

2
Myths and Misunderstandings

The Slade family and their ships have been included in several books. The *Jane Slade*, in particular, is frequently referred to as 'the famous *Jane Slade*'. Until now however, there has been no detailed research on her or the family, so some misunderstanding has been printed.

Captain Peter Avery
Basil Lubbock, in Volume I of his book *The Last of the Windjammers*, refers to the 'The famous *Jane Slade*, Captain Peter Avery which held the record for the fastest passage from St Michaels to Bristol, came from Fowey'. There is no record of a Captain Avery in Lloyd's Captains' Register or in the Registers of Certificates of Competency for Masters and Mates (BT122). There is however a Peter Avery who served on the Jane Slade as an Ordinary Seaman aged 18 in 1871.

The Slades of Appledore
Captain WJ Slade wrote an excellent description of his and his father's lives as owners and masters of coastal schooners trading from North Devon (Out of Appledore), but they never built ships for themselves. There is no family linkage between the Slades of Pelynt and Polruan and those of Appledore as was confirmed in correspondence with a descendant, Mr. David Carter.

Trades, Ownership and Builders
Basil Greenhill's superb book *The Merchant Schooners* has been a constant inspiration. However, as has been shown here, the largest vessel built in Fowey, the ES Hocken, was built by Slade and not, by Butson. Secondly, the *Jane Slade* carried more than just an 'occasional fruit cargo' as was suggested by Benjamin Tregaskes. At no stage did the *Jane Slade* enter the Newfoundland trade, concentrating predominantly in her early years on fruit from the Mediterranean, Azores and Bahamas. Finally, she was never owned in Newquay. William Geake was the managing owner (the person appointed to manage the finances of the ship and her shares) for many years, majority share ownership was always held by the Slade family and her registration remained at Fowey, until 1929.

Bankruptcy
It has long been said that the firm became bankrupt after the loss of the AB Sherman. Partly due to Samuel's careful handling of his inheritance from Jane, the firm was able to reach an agreement with its creditors and was therefore able to stay in operation on its main site in Polruan. There was, at this time a bankruptcy of a Slade and Sons, which was in the London Gazette. On investigation they turned out to be a firm of butchers on the Isle of Wight.

J Slade and Sons
From time to time, commentators have referred to John Slade and Sons. It does not seem to have occurred to them that the firm was named after a woman. The initial 'J' always referred to Jane from the time she took over until the end of the firm in 1929. When her grandson, Christopher, was apprenticed in 1877, the certificate was signed by William Salt Slade on behalf of 'J. Slade and Sons'. John was never in sole ownership of the yard. When he took over the yard after the death of Jane and the retirement of William, he did so in partnership with Samuel. Later Samuel was in partnership with Ernie, Jim and Joe.

3
Slade Vessels

Date	Name	Rig	Ton	Dimensions
1856	Peter & James	Brigantine	156	L 92/B 22.7/D 12.5

Lost with all hands in 1865 on passage from Salonika to UK

| 1858 | Kate and Ann | Schooner | 124 | L 86.5/ B 21.9/ D 11.8 |

Sunk after collision with SS Bovonia off Milford Haven 22 Nov 1892. Since raised and used as barge at Milford (22. 5. 1974)

| 1864 | Juno | Schooner | 133 | L 87.4/B 22.3/D 11.8 |

Lost by collision mid-channel near Beachy Head 3 crew lost 2 Mar 1881

| 1866 | Sparkling Wave | Schooner | 154 | L 98.8/B 22.7/D 12.1 |

1882 From Aruba to Hamburg . Was abandoned 23rd July in Lat 68n Long 20w

| 1868 | Silver Stream | Schooner | 163 | L 100.2/B 22.7/D 12.7 |

Lost on voyage from Cadiz to St Johns with a cargo of salt. Posted missing 22 July 1882. Missing since 23 Sept 1881.

| 1870 | Jane Slade | Schooner | 159 | L 97.7/B 22.9/ D 12.3 |

Broken up 20th December 1928

| 1872 | Snowflake | Schooner | 156.6 | L 99.2/B 22.7/D 12.7 |

From Goole to Plymouth Missing 5 July 1882 .Cargo Coals Sailed from Grimsby 29 April. Owner Frank Parkyn

| 1874 | Silver Spray | Schooner | 175.52 | L100.6/B 23.3/D 12.9 |

Sank in Plymouth Sound 30th Dec 1905

| 1877 | Koh-I-Noor | Barquentine | 242.71 | L 120.2/B 25.3/D 12.9 |

Captain William Smith. Ship lost in 1906 by stranding on a reef at the entrance of Boca St Nicoleas Aruba, Netherlands West Indies, off the coast of Venezuela

| 1879 | ES Hocken | Barquentine | 296 | L 126.2/B 25.5/D 13.9 |

Abandoned on December 15 1917 in the North Atlantic, 23.25N 48.17W.

| 1886 | May Queen | Fishing boat | | |

Royal Cornwall Gazette May 7th 1886

| 1888 | Foam | Yacht | 14 | L43.6 / B 11.05/D6.77 |

Still on yacht register 1958

1907	Lucy B	Yacht	13	
1910	Clarice	Yacht	17.03	
1911	Cornubia/Hirta	Pilot cutter	33	

Featured in BBC documentary "Island Race" 1995. Now at Gloucester Docks

| 1922 | Maya | | | |

Boat 18 feet Cost £90 for JH Samuel. Sold 3 yrs later to Freddy Johns for £100

| 1928 | Majub | Yacht | 10 | L 31/B 10.1/D 4.6 |

Built for Captain Collins, Harbourmaster

| 1929 | Marie-Louise | Yacht | 12.16 | L 32.8/B 10.8/D 7 |

Sold to Frederick Albert Devenish of Croydon 18.7.1932

4
Shareholders in Slade-built Ships

Name	Occupation	Residence	Ships
John Alfred	Gentleman	St Austell	*Koh I Noor*
Richard Barrett	Sailmaker	Polruan	*Peter & James, Juno*

Name	Occupation	Residence	Ships
John Bawden	Cabinet maker	St Austell	*Jane Slade, Snowflake,Silver Spray*
William Beale	Master Mariner	Fowey	*Juno*
James Best	Yeoman	Lanteglos	*Silver Spray*
Charles William Bradhurst	Accountant	St Austell	*Koh I Noor*
Robert Bulgin	Shipbroker	Swansea	*Juno*
Richard Clogg	Butcher	Polruan	*Silver Stream, Jane Slade, Silver Spray, Koh I Noor*
Thomas Cobbledick	Butcher	Fowey	*Kate & Ann*
Jane Louisa Courtis	Wife of Ret master mariner	St Agnes	*ES Hocken*
Nicholas Hicks Dingle	Master Mariner	Polruan	*Koh I Noor*
Thomas Doney	Lighterman	Lerrin	*Kate & Ann*
William Ede	Gentleman	St Veep	*Kate & Ann,Silver Stream, Snowflake*
Em Elford	Yeoman	St Tudy	*Kate & Ann*
William Geake	Schoolmaster/ gentleman	St Columb/ Dobwalls	*Jane Slade Kate & Ann, Silver Stream*
Wesley Grose	Yeoman	St Kew	*Juno*
William Guy	Land Agent	St Veep (note 3)	*Kate & Ann, Juno*
Catherine Harris	Spinster	Polruan	*Koh I Noor*
John Hawken	Blacksmith	Polruan	*Juno, Jane Slade,Snowflake*
James Hayes	Innkeeper	Bodinnick	*Sparkling Wave*
Samuel Hender	Licensed victualler	Bodmin	*ES Hocken*
Ann Hicks	Widow	Fowey	*Koh I Noor, ES Hocken*
John Hicks	Yeoman	Lanteglos	*Jane Slade*
Mary Ann Hicks	Spinster	Polruan	*Peter & James*
William Hicks	Merchant	Fowey	*Juno*
Edward Geake Hocken	Gentleman	Polruan	*Sparkling Wave*
Edward Hocken	Master Mariner	Polruan	*Kate & Ann, Sparkling Wave*
John Edward Hocken	Merchant	Polruan	*Sparkling Wave*
John Edward Hocken	Sailmaker	Polruan	*Jane Slade, Snowflake, Koh I Noor*
John Henry Hocken	Master Mariner	Fowey	*Kate & Ann,Sparkling Wave Snowflake,Silver Spray, ES Hocken*
Nathaniel Hocken	Master Mariner	Polruan	*Snowflake,Silver Spray, ES Hocken*
William Pearce Hocken	Master Mariner	Fowey	*Kate & Ann, Sparkling Wave*
Wm Henry Hony	Banker	Lostwithiel	*Snowflake*
John Jenkins	Coastguard	Polruan	*ES Hocken*
Nicholas Johns	Yeoman	Tywardreath	*Kate & Ann*
Joseph Jorey	Merchant	Pentewan	*Sparkling Wave*
Henry Lamb	Draper	Fowey	*Peter & James, Kate & Ann*
Richard Langmaid	Ship carpenter	Cardiff	*Sparkling Wave*
Alfred Lidgey	Accountant	Truro	*Sparkling Wave*
Alfred Luke	Merchant	Charlestown	*Koh I Noor*
William Henry Luke	Merchant	Charlestown	*Koh I Noor*
William Luke	Merchant	Charlestown	*Sparkling Wave, Silver Stream, Jane Slade*
Thomas Mark	Master Mariner	Polruan	*Peter & James*
John Martin	Innkeeper farmer/yeoman	Fowey	*ES Hocken Silver Stream, Jane Slade*
Joseph C Martyn	Master Mariner	Polruan	*Peter & James*
William Morcom	Innkeeper	Par	*Koh I Noor*
Thomas Mutton	Butcher	Lerrin	*Juno, Jane Slade*
Francis Nickle	Yeoman	Helland	*Kate & Ann*

Name	Occupation	Residence	Ships
William Nine	Merchant	Fowey	*ES Hocken*
Thomas Northcott	Yeoman	Pelynt	*Silver Spray, ES Hocken*
John Olford	Merchant	Lostwithiel	*Silver Stream, Snowflake*
John Oliver	Yeoman	Fowey	*ES Hocken*
James Palmer	Farmer	Duloe	*Koh I Noor*
Elford Parkyn	Merchant	Lostwithiel	*Kate & Ann*
Frank Parkyn	Merchant	Lerrin	*Kate & Ann, Snowflake*
Thomas Pearce	Yeoman	St Blazey	*Juno, Jane Slade, Snowflake, Silver Spray, Koh I Noor, ES Hocken*
William Edward Pearce	Yeoman	St Blazey	*Koh I Noor*
Albert Pearn	Master Mariner	Polruan	*Silver Spray*
William Phillips	Merchant	St Austell	*ES Hocken*
William Hy. Polybank	Gentleman	Stoke, Devonport	*Snowflake*
Richard Reed	Merchant	Lostwithiel	*ES Hocken*
John Robertson	Shipowner	Grangemouth	*Peter & James*
Charles Rowe	Master Mariner	Polruan	*Sparkling Wave, Silver Stream*
Richard Rundle	Auctioneer	Lostwithiel	*Koh I Noor*
Elizabeth Salt	Widow	Polruan	*Jane Slade*
Philip Salt	Master Mariner	Polruan	*Sparkling Wave*
William Merrifield Scantlebury	Draper	St Veep, Lerrin	*Snowflake*
Thomas Sherwill	Gentleman	Lostwithiel	*ES Hocken*
Samuel Short	Yeoman	Fowey	*Juno*
John Slade	Innkeeper	Pelynt	*Koh I Noor*
Elizabeth Smith	Widow	Fowey	*Koh I Noor*
William Smith	Ret Master Mariner	Polruan	*Koh I Noor*
William Sobey	Attorney at Law	Fowey	*Juno*
Fanny Stephens	Grocer	Polruan	*Jane Slade, Snowflake*
George Stephens	Yeoman	Liskeard	*Kate & Ann*
Nathaniel Stephens	Yeoman	St Tudy	*Kate & Ann,*
Nehemiah Stephens	Yeoman	Liskeard	*Sparkling Wave, Silver Stream, Jane Slade, Snowflake, ES Hocken*
William Stephens	Grocer	Polruan	*Silver Stream*
Francis Edward Stocken	Ironmonger	St Austell	*ES Hocken*
Elias Roskilly Tadd	Master Mariner	Polruan	*Silver Stream, Jane Slade*
Peter Tadd	Shipowner	Polruan	*Peter & James*
Sam Roskilly Tadd	Master Mariner	Polruan	*Silver Stream*
Samuel Tadd	Master Mariner	Polruan	*Snowflake*
John Thomas	Weslyan Minister	Stow in the Wold	*ES Hocken*
Edward John Treffry	Gentleman	Fowey	*Kate & Ann, Sparkling Wave, Silver Stream*
Nicholas Tregaskes	Merchant	Polruan	*Silver Stream*
George Robert Truscott	Yeoman	Triggabrowne	*ES Hocken*
Charles Varcoe	Yeoman	Lanteglos	*Juno*
Richard Harris Williams	Civil Engineer	Cuddra House	*Koh I Noor*
Thomas Wyatt	Shipwright	Polruan	*Silver Stream*

Source: Port of Fowey Registration Books
Notes:
1. Date is as date of registration of vessel
2. Occupation and address is as at first registration
3. Later noted as of High Wycombe

5
Slade Family Shareholdings in other Ships
Share Details(note 1)

Ship's Name	FoweyReg date	Built	Rig	Tons
Charlotte & Hannah	1834	Polruan by Geach	Schooner	75
1855 C Slade 4 shares (Wrecked Pentewan 1857)				
Levant Star	1836	Merioneth 1819	Snow	146
C Slade 2 shares (Sold to Exeter 1839)				
Ranger	1839	Fowey by Rendle	Sloop	53
C Slade 4 shares				
Rachel Ann	1841	Fowey by Rendle	Schooner	66
C Slade 4 shares				
Alert	1842	Polruan by Butson	Schooner	68
C Slade 36 sh.1861 C Slade 46 (Mng owner) Thomas Slade 4. Jane inherits and sells to Chas Lobb in May 1870				
Brilliant	1850	1835 Franks Quarry,Devon	Schooner	68
C Slade 18. (Ship sold in 1853)				
Capella	1856	PEI	Brigantine	122
C Slade 4 sh. 1858 Shares sold to W S Slade (Conv to coal hulk 1888)				
Fancy	1825	Polruan by Geach	Sloop	47
C Slade 2 sh in 1842. Sells all shares in 1860				
Isabella	1865	1864 Galmpton,Dartmouth	Schooner	60
C Slade 4 sh. Jane inherits plus 2 sh. from W Salt. (Lost 1913)				
Concord	1858	PEI 1857	Brigantine	133
Jane buys 4 sh in 1871 (Lost off Holyhead in 1884)				
Kingaloch	1861	Wallace,Nova Scotia	Brigantine	122
Jane buys 4 sh in 1871 (Lost on passage Fowey to Newcastle 1883)				
Wild Wave	1861	PEI	Brigantine	160
C Slade 2 sh. Inherited by Jane then Samuel				
Jane & Ann	1865	Newburgh,Fifeshire	Brigantine	160
C Slade 2 sh				
Mary Helen	1857	Ramsgate	Schooner	98
C Slade 2 sh. Jane inherits (ship lost 1888)				
Adelaide	1869	Padstow	Brigantine	164
Jane buys 3 sh 1877Samuel inherits 3 and buys 2 more sh in 1892				
Gem	1871	Polruan by Butson	Brigantine	163
Oct. 95 E C Slade buys 2 and Samuel buys 2				
Calenick	1872	Llanelly 1826	Brigantine	126
Jane buys 4. Sold foreign in 1878				
Sir Robert Hodgson	1872	PEI 1869	Brig	203
Jane buys 2 sh				
Ocean Traveller	1872	Appledore 1872	Brigantine	198
Jane buys 1 in 1872 (Lost in Caribean sea in 1878)				
Lady Ernestine	1873	Cremyll 1869	Schooner	138
Jane buys 2 sh				
Alexandrina	1873	Buckie, Banff 1866	Schooner	89
Jane buys 2 sh. (Lost Nth Wales 1890)				
Lydia Cardell	1873	Appledore, 1873	Brigantine	224
John Slade 2 sh. 9.4.01 sells to Tyrrell of Arklow 29.7.1903				
Ontario	1874	PEI 1873	Brigantine	166
S Slade managing owner				

Ship's Name	FoweyReg date	Built	Rig	Tons
Louise Charlotte	1876	Stralsund, Germany 1849	Schooner	113
Jane buys 4 sh 4.5.77. (Converted to hospital hulk 1885)				
Ada Peard	1875	Par	Brigantine	256
T H Slade 8 in 1906 Sells 4 to James Sydney Slade				
Martha Edmonds	1878	Milford, Pembroke 1873	Brig	186
John Slade 2 sh Aug 1908				
Gudrun	1882	Varazze, Italy 1874	Brigantine	243
Thomas Slade 2 sh 4.7.82				
Amy A Lane	1890	Seaport, Maine, USA 1867	Brigantine	425
Samuel Slade 2 sh 19.10.92. (Sold to Sweden 19.11.1894)				
Amy	1890	Banff 1870 by Watson	Schooner	133
Blown up and sunk during filming operations 10.9.28.Date of advice from Robert Henry Adams beneficial owner				
Trevellas	1918	St Agnes, Hayle 1876	Schooner	127
E C Slade 64 sh. Sells most shares to Kearon family by 1925				
Thames	1923	Plymouth 1875	Brigantine	177
E C Slade 64 sh. Sold in 1924				

Source: Port of Fowey Ships Registers
Note 1. Date of share purchase is date of Fowey registration unless otherwise stated

6
Atlantic Passages of *Jane Slade*, Master Thomas Slade

Pss'ge (note:1)	Outport		Inport		Est. days (note:2)
1	Cardiff	30-Dec-70	Palermo	19-Jan-71	
2	Palermo	19-Feb-71	New York	13-Apr-71	53
3	New York	22-Apr-71	Dunkirk	12-Jun-71	51
4	Dunkirk	15-Jun-71	Fowey	27-Jun-71	
1	Newcastle	08-Feb-72	Fowey	27-Feb-72	
2	Fowey	27-Feb-72	Milazzo	29-Mar-72	
3	Milazzo	29-Mar-72	Palermo	02-Apr-72	
4	Palermo	02-Apr-72	Philadelphia	28-May-72	56
5	Philadelphia	10-Jun-72	Belfast	09-Jul-72	29
1	Hamburg	01-Feb-73	Palermo	04-Apr-73	
2	Palermo	25-Apr-73	New York	25-Jun-73	61
3	New York	03-Jul-73	Newry	05-Aug-73	33
1	Cardiff	05-Feb-74	Palermo	08-Mar-74	
2	Palermo	10-Apr-74	New York	13-Jun-74	64
3	New York	13-Jul-74	Corfu	16-Aug-74	34
4	Corfu	6-Aug-74	Gallipolli	27-Aug-74	
5	Gallipoll	i27-Aug-74	Susa	18-Sep-74	
6	Susa	18-Sep-74	Glasgow	03-Nov-74	
1	Fowey	17-Oct-76	Rochefort	22-Oct-76	
2	Rochefort	03-Nov-76	St Michaels	17-Nov-76	14
3	St Michaels	09-Dec-76	Hull	23-Dec-76	14

Pss'ge (note:1)	Outport		Inport		Est. days (note:2)
1	Sligo	29-Jan-78	Curacao	25-Mar-78	55
2	Curacao	25-Mar-78	Hull	20-May-78	56
1	Hull	10-Oct-78	Rio Grande	03-Oct-79(note:3)	
2	Rio Grande	03-Nov-79	Buenos Aires	17-Nov-79	
3	B Aires	02-Jan-80	Liverpool	07-Jun-80	156
1	Newport	13-Jan-82	St Michaels	15-Feb-82	33
2	St Michaels	06-Mar-82	London	27-Mar-82	21
1	Fowey	22-Jun-82	Trieste	05-Aug-82	
2	Trieste	14-Aug-82	Barletta	19-Aug-82	
3	Barletta	27-Aug-82	Lisbon	08-Oct-82	
4	Lisbon	19-Oct-82	St Michaels	04-Nov-82	16
5	St Michaels	16-Nov-82	London	30-Nov-82	14
1	London	10-Dec-82	Newcastle	13-Dec-82	
2	S Shields	27-Dec-82	St Michaels	28-Jan-83	32
3	St Michaels	08-Feb-83	Bristol	24-Feb-83	18
1	Bristol	13-Mar-83	La Guayra	30-Apr-83	48
2	La Guayra	10-May-83	Aruba	17-May-83	
3	Aruba	25-May-83	Hamburg	13-Jul-83	49
4	Hamburg	24-Jul-83	Sth Shields	04-Aug-83	
1	Fowey	22-Sep-83	Seville	10-Oct-83	
2	Seville	16-Oct-83	St Michaels	01-Nov-83	16
3	St Michaels	20-Nov-8 3	London	04-Dec-83	14
1	London	06-Dec-83	St Michaels	31-Dec-83	25
2	St Michaels	22-Jan-84	Bristol	09-Feb-84	16
1	Bristol	25-Feb-84	Demerara	05-Apr-84	39
2	Demerara	09-May-84	Bristol	24-Jun-84	46
1	Bristol	2-Jul-84	Fowey	06-Jul-84	
2	Fowey	11-Aug-84	Leith	21-Aug-84	
3	Leith	05-Sep-84	Fecamp	10-Sep-84	
4	Fecamp	24-Oct-84	Fowey	02-Oct-84	
	St Michaels	unknown	Bristol	08-Dec-84 (note:4)	
1	Bristol	31-Dec-84	St Michaels	15-Jan-85	15
2	St Michaels	14-Feb-85	London	28-Feb-85	14
1	Fowey	21-Mar-85	Cat Island	03-May-85	41
2	Cat Island	10-Jun-85	London	15-Jul-85	35
1	Fowey	29-Sep-85	St Michaels	17-Oct-85	18
2	St Michaels	05-Nov-85	London	28-Nov-85	23
1	Cardiff	06-Jan-86	Terceira, Azores	01-Feb-86	26
2	Terceira	12-Feb-86	Barbados	21-Mar-86	
3	Barbados	26-Mar-86	St Kitts	29-Apr-86	
4	St Kitts	29-Apr-86	London	12-Jun-86	44

Pss'ge (note:1)	Outport		Inport		Est. days (note:2)
1	Falmouth	04-Aug-86	Malta	10-Sep-86	
2	Malta	20-Sep-86	St Michaels	17-Oct-86	27
3	St Michaels	15-Nov-86	Bristol	29-Nov-86	14
1	Fowey	03-Sep-87	Leghorn	01-Oct-87	
2	Leghorn	11-Oct-87	St Michaels	30-Nov-87	50
3	St Michaels	14-Dec-87	Bristol	09-Jan-88	26
1	Cardiff	29-Feb-88	Dakar	19-Apr-88	50
2	Dakar	19-Apr-88	Rum Cay	06-May-88	17
3	Rum Cay	02-Jun-88	London	12-Jul-88	40
1	Fowey	09-Apr-89	San Salvador	15-May-89	37
2	San Salvador/Cat Island	11-Jun-89	London	11-Jul-89	30

Notes:
1. Each group of passages is one crew agreement and all passages are given for completeness
2. Dates are from the consulate date stamps or Customs Bills of entry
3. Clearly she went elsewhere between these dates, but there is no information
4. No crew agreement, but dates are from Customs Bills
Source : Crew agreements and Customs Bills

7
Examples of cargoes of *Jane Slade*, Master Thomas Slade

Year	Date arr	Port	Outport	Broker	Cargo
1874	1st Jan	Bristol	Catania etc	Pike	80t brimstone 682 bgs seed Order @ Palermo 1456 bgs shumac Order
1876	23rd Dec	Hull	St Michaels	White	2184 pkgs oranges, 4 pineapples
1878	21st May	Hull	Curacoa	Woodhead	260t phosphate rock
1878	20th Sept	Hull	Marseilles	Hammond	260t oilcake
1880	12th Nov	Hull	Gallipoli	Hammond	189 cks oil
1880	8th June	Liverpool	Paysandu	Hicks	7940 wet salted ox hides, 7000 Horns, 13t horn pith Order
1882	25th Mar	London	St Michaels	Tatham & Co	2191 bxs oranges 58bxs tangerines 24 pkgs pines 7 pkgs bananas Order
1882	30th Nov	London	St Michaels	Tatham & Co	2028 pkg oranges 10 bunches bananas 1093 pineapples 20 bxs potatoes Order
1883	26th Feb	Bristol	St Michaels	Chessell	2254 pkg oranges 58 pkgs pines Order
1883	4th Dec	London	St Michaels	Tatham & Co	21 pkgs tangerines 147 pkgs pineapples 2881 pkgs oranges 1 pkg bananas Order
1884	14th Feb	Bristol	St Michaels	Chessell	2193 pkgs oranges 24 pkags pines Order
1884	26th June	Bristol	Demerara	Chessell	162 hds 29 tcs 50 brls sugar 61 pns rum 6700 cocoa nuts Order
1884	8th Dec	Bristol	St Michaels	Chessell & Co	2186 bx oranges 72 bxs pines 21 bxs potatoes 2 cr bananas 3 bxs tangerines

Year	Date arr	Port	Outport	Broker	Cargo
1885	14th July	London	Cat Island	Tatham & Co	3390 dz pineapples
1886	28th Feb	London	St Michaels	Tatham & Co	1708 pk oranges 92 pk tangerines 154 pk pineapples 9 pk potatoes 2 pk pumpkins Order
1886	15th June	London	Charlestown W I		360 hds 279 brls sugar 25 brls tamarinds 10300 cocao nuts 1 pk maize C Neilsen
1886	2nd Dec	Bristol	St Michaels	Chessell	1959 bxs oranges 81 bxs pines 3 bxs bananas
1888	12th Jan	Bristol	St Michaels	Chessell	2127 bxs oranges 77 pkg pines 1 pkg tangerines
1888	13th July	London	Rum Cay	Tatham Bromage	2000 dx pineapples Order
1888	22nd Dec	London	Messina	T Nelson & Son	2683 cases lemons Castell & Brown
1889	11th July	London	Cat Island	Tatham Bromage	3000 dz pineapples
1890	5th Aug	Bristol	Tatza	Chessell	170t valonia
1891	30 th May	Bristol	Corfu	Chessell	369 cks oil

Sources: H. M. Customs Bills of Entry for Liverpool, Hull, London, Bristol

8
Masters and Managing Owners

Masters of the *Jane Slade*

October 1870 to April 1892	Thomas Slade
May 1892 to January 1894	Thomas Herbert Slade
January 1894 to November 1894	James Sydney Slade
January 1896 to August 1899	Adam Veale (Newquay)
November 1899 to February 1903	George Thomas (Port Isaac)
February 1903 to June 1910	John Andrews (Liverpool)
June 1910 to August 1914	P M Jacobs (Polruan)
September 1914 to December 1918	Henry David Smith (Chester)
December 1918 to January 1919	Ben Williams (Cardiff)
January 1919 to June 1920	H Cohring (Arklow)
June 1920 to August 1923	G Kearon (Arklow)
August 1923 to November 1924	W H Cort (Jersey)

Managing Owners

1870 to 1872	Jane S Slade
1873 to 1893	William Geake
1893 to 1910	Thomas Slade
1910 to 1928	E C Slade

Last crew paid off 12th November 1924
Ship removed from Port of Fowey Register December 1928

9
Sources and Selected Bibliography

Primary sources

Census returns for Lanteglos by Fowey, Pelynt and Fowey. Cornwall County Record Office
Parish Registers of baptism, burials and marriages for Lanteglos by Fowey, Pelynt and Fowey. Cornwall County Record Office
Land Tax Assessments 1838 to 1871. Cornwall County Record Office Ref X 186/1
List of Ships and shipbuilders for Port of Fowey. Extracted from Cornwall Maritime Museum Ships Database. Courtesy of Captain G. Hogg, Hon. Curator
Masters certificates of competency. National Maritime Museum Greenwich
Port Registration Books of Fowey. Cornwall County Record Office
Wills. Cornwall County Record Office, Bodmin Probate Registry
St Lawrences (County Asylum) Visitors Minute Book. Cornwall County Record Office
Lloyds Captains Register. Guildhall Library, London
Crew Lists and Agreements. National Maritime Museum, St Johns University, Newfoundland, Cornwall County Record Office
Fowey Pilots Ms30198. Guildhall Library London
Tithe Map and list of owners and occupiers for Polruan in 1841. Cornwall County Record Office
Kellys Directories. Cornish Studies Library Redruth
Pigotts Directory of Cornwall. Royal Institution of Cornwall Library
Post Office Directory. Royal Institution of Cornwall Library
Slaters Directory. Royal Institution of Cornwall Library
Universal British Directory 1793-98. Royal Institution of Cornwall Library

Bibliography

Ackland, NA and Druce RM (1978) *Lanteglos by Fowey: The Story of a Parish* Fowey
Bartlett, John (1996) *Ships of North Cornwall* Tabb House
Barton, RM. (1966) *A History of the Cornish China Clay Industry* Bradford Barton
Barton, RM. (1966) *Life in Cornwall in the 19th Century* 4. Vols (extracts from the West Briton) Bradford Barton
Bainbridge, George (1980) *The Wooden ships and iron men of the Cornish china clay industry* Charlestown
Bouquet,Michael (1980) *Westcountry Sail* David & Charles
Dewar-Brown, W (1962) 'The Little Ships of Troy' series of nine articles, *The Cornish Magazine* March to Nov
Doe, Helen (1998) 'Shipbuilders and the Community, Polruan 1841-1871' in *Maritime South West* No 11 Journal of the South West Maritime History Society
Doe, Helen (2001) 'Politics, Property and Family Resources' *Family and Community History Journal* Vol 3 No 1 Maney
Greenhill, Basil (1950 & 1988) *The Merchant Schooner* Conway
Greenhill, Basil & Ann Gifford (1974) *Westcountrymen in Prince Edward's Isle* Toronto University Press
Greenhill, Basil(ed) (1993) *Sail's Last Century*. Conway
Grigson, Geoffrey (1954) *Freedom of the Parish* Phoenix
Harrison, J.F.C.(1988) *Early Victorian Britain 1832-1851* Fontana Press
Hudson, Kenneth (1970) *The History of English China Clays* David & Charles
Keast, John (1950) *The Story of Fowey* Dyllansow Truran
Keast, John (1982) *The King of Mid Cornwall The Life of Joseph Thomas Treffry (1782-1850)* Dyllansow Truran
Keast, John (1987) *The Book of Fowey* Barracuda
Lubbock, Basil (1929) *The Last of the Windjammers* 2 Vols. Brown, Son & Ferguson Glasgow
Macgregor, David (1984) *Merchant Sailing Ships 1850-1875* Conway
Parkes, C (2000) Fowey Estuary Historic Audit (Cornwall Archaeological Unit)
Pickering, Isabel (1993) *Pictures of a Parish* Fowey

Pickering, Isabel (1995) *Some Goings on! A selection of newspaper articles about Fowey, Polruan and Lanteglos districts from 1800 –1899* Fowey

Pickering, Isabel (1997) *Back-a Long. Memories of Lanteglos by Fowey* Fowey

Richards, John 'Bygone Polruan' Article in Old Cornwall Vol VIII No 9

Slaven, A (1980) 'The Shipbuilding Industry' in Church, R (Ed.) *The Dynamics of Victorian Business* George Allen and Unwin

Stammers, Michael (1998) 'A 19th century shipyard model from Wells-Next-The-Sea' in Norfolk Archaeology

Ward-Jackson, CH (1980) ' Stephens of Fowey' *Maritime Monographs and Reports*, National Maritime Museum

Ward-Jackson, CH (1986) *Ships and Shipbuilders of a Westcountry Seaport. Fowey 1786-1939* Twelveheads Press

SELECTIVE INDEX OF PEOPLE AND PLACES

SHIP INDEX